Something More?

Something More?

Miracles in the Bible ... and how they impact us

Stephen Bishop

Published by Bible-Bish-Books
London E10 6DW
www.bible-bish-books.co.uk

Published 2023

ISBN 978-1-7399482-2-1

Cover picture: Stixwould Station - Lincolnshire

Contents

Section Two: God's intervention - signposts
Looking at some of the miracles of Jesus - what they reveal about His power to work in our lives in different ways

Introduction

"You are the God who performs miracles; you display your power among the peoples." (Psalm 77:14)

Read: Psalm 77

'More red tape!'

This was the unspoken reaction of Herbert White to his visitor's comment. The latter was a local doctor who, like Herbert, was a committed Christian. Herbert had shown him around the house that he, helped by his wife and other supporters, had opened as an orphanage. At the dawn of the last century such an undertaking was a huge task. There was no government or local authority provision or resourcing for the care of children who had lost their parents either through death or desertion. Mortality rates were high in an era before the National Health Service was formed, and only limited medical care was available for the working classes. But Herbert White, conscious of the need of many such children in that area on the London and Essex border, sensed that God had called him to provide a home for those now left on their own.

Total trust

Herbert, in addition, believed that this meant resigning from his job in a bank in order to give his whole time and energy to this task - his manager thought him mad to take such a step. And there was a further belief that he held. From the outset he had been sure that God wanted him to trust Him totally for all the essentials, everything from premises to staff, food, clothing and utensils. So without any form of advertising, promotion or canvasing, the needs of this new home had been met by God's provision.

A further need!

But that was until now. The doctor's comments suddenly brought to Herbert's awareness a further need that had to be addressed. He had explained that this home in South Woodford (which was eventually named 'Mill Grove' some years later) should have a medical officer. This would ensure the ongoing provision of healthcare and medical oversight of the large number of children being cared for - over sixty of them - as well as for the staff and Herbert's own family. Herbert's spirits dropped as he heard this. Finding a medical practitioner willing to take such responsibility, and the cost of their services, would be another huge aspect of running the home.

Not quite finished!

However Dr Flegg, the name of this local doctor, having been shown round the Home and coming back to speak to Herbert about this further need, had not quite finished! Without Herbert saying anything the doctor added that not only would he offer his own services as the Home's medical officer but that he would do so free of charge. In addition he would be available 24/7 and medication would be provided at no cost!

God's miraculous provision of finance for the Home, coming through the spontaneous contributions of local and other Christians, now extended to something more. Because, following Dr Flegg's conviction that this role was something that God had called him to undertake, he subsequently served in this way for thirty-three years. He was thereby responsible for the well-being of over 600 children during that period, dealing with a wide range of ailments. Yet he told Herbert that he was the one who benefited most from this responsibility.

A 'snapshot' ...

This account constitutes a 'snapshot' of God's work and intervention beyond our own conception or resourcing. It reflects His care and understanding as our Heavenly Father. The provision by God in situations where we have neither the means nor the ingenuity to bring any kind of resolution by ourselves, nor from others, points us firmly to His miraculous ways of working.

This term 'miraculous' is one with which some may feel uncomfortable. There have been many 'miracles' that have proved to be false or exaggerated. Yet the Bible clearly records God's work in such ways. These frequently lack the blaze of publicity or hype that can be associated with such intervention. Most of them are low key and almost unobtrusive. But they show God's compassion for people who realised their own powerlessness, and their desperate need for Him to act.

... some serious questions ...

Asaph, who wrote some of the Psalms, clearly recorded such need, and God's response in Psalm 77. He raised serious questions similar to those we ask when confronted with crises. Where is God? What is He doing? Why doesn't He intervene?

Although his circumstances were very different to ours his desperate plight and lack of control over situations that were engulfing him were factors with which we can identify. His reaction was to turn to God: *"When I was in distress, I sought the Lord; at night I stretched out untiring hands, and I would not be comforted"* (verse 2). Asaph recognised that he needed God's intervention but could not see any response to his prayer, hence those desperate questions: *"Will the Lord reject for ever? Will he never show his favour again? Has his unfailing love vanished for ever? Has his promise failed for all time? Has God forgotten to be merciful? Has he in anger withheld his compassion?"*

... a statement ...

But as the psalmist stood with a sense of powerlessness he remembered what God had done in the past. This was in respect of His powerful intervention in releasing the oppressed Israelites from Egyptian slavery, and making a way for them through the parted Red Sea (verses 16-19). He prefaced this recollection: *"I will remember the deeds of the LORD; yes, I will remember your miracles of long ago. I will consider all your works...your mighty deeds"* (verses 11-12). He then made a clear and unequivocal statement: *"You are the God who performs miracles..."* The focus of those miracles was also stated *"...you display your power among the peoples"* (verse 14). This was the 'destination' at which Asaph realised he needed to aim as the answer to his anguished questions. The events of the Exodus many centuries earlier pointed towards it - God's powerful intervention. And Asaph was giving no room for debate, discussion, dispute or doubt regarding God being able to work miraculously again.

... sitting well? ...

But such a statement does not sit well in our own times. Consensus, popular opinion, social media postings and 'conversations' are seen as setting the direction of our attitudes, expectations and belief systems. So a conviction that God works by way of *"mighty deeds...who performs miracles"* is contested and denied by many in our contemporary culture. It is particularly countered by the rationalism, humanism, agnosticism, secularism, cynicism and scepticism that exists around us, pumped out by major media sources. So it's not surprising that many Christians are anaesthetised, apathetic or ambivalent with regard to the possibility that God is still able and wants to *"perform miracles"* in our lives. The battering, bruising, bewilderment and brokenness of life have also left their mark, particularly arising from the Pandemic and associated lockdowns. This has left a substantial number of Christians in 'survival mode', having little expectation of change by way of God's intervention.

... *"signs"* ...

These are persuasive reasons why God's *"...deeds... miracles ...works"* need to be underlined for us in this present day together with the ways in which we can make 'space' to respond to what He is able to do. That is the thrust of this book. **Section One** reflects on God's miraculous intervening power through Elisha the prophet, recorded in the Old Testament. His name means 'God is salvation' or 'God saves,' and the accounts involving him can be seen as 'setting the scene' for the miracles subsequently performed by Jesus. John specifically labels Jesus' miracles in his Gospel as *"miraculous signs"* (John 2:11) and these (from the Gospel of John, and a selection from Mark) are used as the focus of **Section Two.** These will help us to understand the ways by which God can still intervene in this age, impacting our own lives.

... and 'space'

However there is a particular feature in all these Biblical accounts which needs to be noted. It is an important element drawn out in these reflections. Each miracle brings to light some aspect of how God intervenes by which we can learn to make 'space' for Him to work. We cannot force or manipulate God to act in any particular way, but we can be in a better position to experience His intervention. Listening to what He is saying, being obedient and trusting Him, are responses that are especially relevant. But there are other responses we need to be aware of and to act upon, highlighted in these chapters.

Whilst the details of these miracles involved events many centuries ago they are still relevant, highlighting God's power and compassion. Everyone featured in these interventions needed and somehow looked for 'something more.' Do you?

Author's Note

- The chapters in this book can be approached as 'stand alone' reading - they do not need to be read in sequence.

- They may also provide a source for devotional reading over a period of time.

- The Reflections at the end of each chapter provide an opportunity to pause and think through particular aspects of what has just been read. They can also be used as a basis for group discussion.

- Suggested prayers have been included as part of these Reflections to encourage a greater sense of drawing close to God.

- I also want to acknowledge with gratitude the incidental as well as specific help of friends in terms of input for this material. In that respect I have been particularly assisted by Dan Leighton. The final responsibility for this book, however, rests with me.

- Finally, feedback and comment are welcome. Please get in touch: **biblebish3927@btinternet.com**

SECTION ONE

God's intervention - setting the scene

Looking at the miracles of God through Elisha the prophet - what they show us about making space for Him to work

1. Where is God?

"Where now is the LORD, the God of Elijah?" (2 Kings 2:14)

Read: 2 Kings 2:1-18

Tenacity and persistence. These are not qualities considered 'cool'. Many who are described as 'celebrities' seem to get what they want without needing to break sweat. Are we to anticipate the miraculous intervention of God without any effort on our part ... or is our input needed in some way?

Elisha's role as God's prophet saw him first alongside his mentor Elijah. It was evident that these two men were together for some time. Students from the various *"company of the prophets"* identified Elisha as being under the tutelage of Elijah their leader. Clearly this had been no short-term mission trip, gap-year assignment or brief internship. Having put behind him the prospect of running his family farming business - undoubtedly a lucrative one on account of owning twelve yoke of oxen needed to plough their land - this was now Elisha's chosen path. But in order to experience the intervention of God for himself, Elisha was not going to be a spectator as miracles took place before him. Instead, he was to be intimately involved.

Significant journey

Sticking with Elijah was the initial and vital part of his calling from God which Elisha had to undertake. And he remained with the older prophet to the very end. It was important that Elisha was with him as they visited specific locations.

Reminders

Each of these had significance in the history of God's people, perhaps a reason for there being a *"company of the prophets"* at each one. They could also be seen as a reminder to Elisha of what God was doing in his own life. The first place on their journey was Gilgal. This was where the Israelites had recommitted their lives to God through the rite of circumcision after arriving in the Promised Land following their exodus from Egypt. As a result of this recommitment God spoke of having *"rolled away"* the shame (*"reproach,"* Joshua 5:9) of their slavery. God had dealt with their past - it had been put firmly away in much the same way as Elisha had been called to put his past behind him as he chose to commit himself to God.

Bethel, a name which means *"house of God,"* was the next place this pair of prophets visited. It was the spot where, centuries previously, God had dramatically revealed Himself to the patriarch Jacob whilst on the run from his vengeful older brother. This revelation came in the form of a dream in which God spoke to him from heaven where a stairway reached down to the place where Jacob had laid down to sleep. God promised Jacob that he would be in the continuing line of Abraham's descendants through whom all nations would be blessed (Genesis 28:10-22). It was an important reminder to Elisha that God stuck to His promises however unpromising the situations that were being faced.

Tenacity

Finally Elisha and Elijah came to Jericho. It was well-known as the place where God intervened in an amazing way by reducing to rubble the impregnable walls of that city which had confronted the Israelites as they entered the Promised Land. The Israelites had been directed to march round those walls on each of the first six days, and then seven times on the seventh day before God clearly stepped in. It was a destination that testified to Elisha of God's power being released as He was tenaciously obeyed, even in apparently impossible situations.

Sticking with it

Elisha had been instructed to "*stay here*" at each of these symbolic locations as Elijah undertook what turned out to be his final journey on earth. But Elisha refused to leave him. He was in no doubt as to the significance of what turned out to be Elijah's last day on earth, and what lay at the end of the road that was being travelled. *"When the LORD was about to take Elijah up to heaven in a whirlwind..."* (2 Kings 2:1) was the statement made as the prelude to these events and the dialogue between the two men. The company of the prophets underlined what was going to take place when they asked Elisha: *"Do you know that the LORD is going to take your master from you today?"* (2 Kings 2:3, 5).

But Elisha was determined to stick with Elijah. *"So the two of them walked on."* They eventually arrived at the River Jordan. Even here was a lesson from the past. Not all of the twelve Israelite tribes had chosen to cross this natural barrier to the Promised Land. Two tribes, and half of a third, had decided to remain on the east side of the river rather than battle through and settle in the place God had given to them. That seemed to epitomise the Israelites and the times in which Elisha and Elijah were living. The nation was not only split in a political and geographical sense, but also spiritually. The majority wanted to 'do their own thing'. This was why the lives of these men of God were so important in demonstrating what it meant to stay with God ... and experience His miraculous intervention.

Spiritual inheritance

Elisha's perseverance was severely tested. It was only after he had remained with the older man, having crossed the River Jordan which had miraculously parted, that he was then asked: *"Tell me, what can I do for you before I am taken from you?"* His answer was to request that he *"...inherit a double portion of your spirit"* (2 Kings 2:9). As the eldest son Elisha would have been legally entitled to receive a share of his father's possessions that was twice the size of his younger brother's (Deuteronomy 21:17). By turning his back on his family Elisha may have forfeited this right. So he simply but determinedly requested the spiritual equivalent. *"A difficult thing,"* he was told ... but not impossible. It became a reality when he fulfilled the condition laid down by Elijah, witnessing Elijah's transportation to heaven in a *"chariot of fire."*

Symbol of God's anointing

Elisha then picked up the cloak that had fallen from Elijah as he had ascended to heaven. It was the symbol of God's anointing and gifting which Elisha had doggedly sought. But this was not before he had declared Elijah as being the embodiment of the nation's real strength, as distinct from the military power of the apostate king, in crying out the words: *"My father! My father! The chariots and horsemen of Israel!"* Tearing his clothes was a means of adding force to those words and of mourning the departure of this man of God.

Demonstrated

Having remained faithful to the calling that he had been given, not turning back or giving up, Elisha now demonstrated his belief in the anointing that had come upon him. He asked the rhetorical question, *"Where now is the LORD, the God of Elijah?"* There was a swift response - his striking the waters of the River Jordan and saw them part once more, enabling him to cross as Elijah had previously done.

Persistence was a factor that appeared further on in this account ... but in a negative way! The *"company of the prophets"* from Jericho persisted in requesting permission from Elisha to search for Elijah who they thought could have been picked up by the Spirit of the Lord and put down again in some mountain or valley. Elisha initially refused. But they kept on at him so that he eventually relented. Their subsequent failure to find Elijah resulted in Elisha firmly putting them in their place: *"Didn't I tell you not to go?"*

A building project!

This important element of tenacity and persistence in experiencing God's miraculous intervention was a key factor in the site redevelopment undertaken by my local church, All Saints Woodford Wells. The scheme was a massive one and included the construction of a two-storey annex for youth work, converting the existing hall into office and meeting spaces, and building a coffee shop. It also involved many noughts in the cost! Plans were put together and practical steps taken. Spiritual action was also initiated. Prayer meetings were set up to see this vision brought into reality over the three years of construction.

Problems confronting the project saw God intervene as a result of tenacious and persistent prayer. These interventions included the provision of fine weather when major excavations were taking place, cash-flow issues being resolved, precision positioning of concrete piles for foundation work, and the intricate piecing together of glass panels for the atrium. It was a series of minor miracles (and some pretty major ones!) arising from continuing prayer that resulted in the successful completion of this work.

Seeing the miraculous intervention of God and experiencing something more involves not giving up on what He says we need to do! Are you ready to persevere?

Reflection

1. What is the value of having reminders of God's work and intervention in the past, as indicated by Elisha and Elijah's visits to specified locations?

2. What situations distract you from persevering in following God and His purposes for your life? How does this account of Elisha staying alongside Elijah help in countering such distractions?

3. In what ways can desperate circumstances act as a 'driver' in you turning to God and asking Him to intervene?

4. What situation are you facing in which persistence is needed so that you can be in a 'place' to experience God's intervention?

Pray: Lord God, please give me the strength I need to follow You and persevere in the pathway you have set before me.

2. Honouring

"This is what the Lord says: 'I have healed this water. Never again will it cause death or make the land unproductive." (2 Kings 2:21)

Read: 2 Kings 2:19 - 25

The Maritime Museum in Liverpool has, among its exhibits, a ticket that had been issued to the Rev John Stuart Holden. It was in respect of a voyage that he was to have undertaken following an invitation to preach in the USA. This was clearly a good opportunity to extend his preaching gift, an ability that was subsequently to see him appointed chairman of the well-established Keswick Convention. At the time of the invitation he was vicar of St Paul's, Portman Square, in London.

But his wife, who was due to accompany him, fell ill. Her condition not only prevented her from being able to travel, but resulted in Stuart Holden making a decision to cancel the journey to the USA as he considered he needed to stay and look after her. Although it meant he was missing out on a big opportunity, he was honouring the commitment and responsibility he had for his spouse which took priority.

But there was an unforeseen factor that emerged in terms of that decision. At that time the only way of travelling across the Atlantic was by ocean liner - air travel was still in its infancy. However Stuart Holden's cancellation of his first class ticket as he resolved to show love and care for his spouse was actually God's miraculous intervention. Because he was due to sail on a ship undertaking its maiden voyage .... the RMS Titanic!

Problems at Jericho!

The Old Testament account concerning Elisha shows that respecting and honouring are important attitudes. They also have longstanding effects. Elisha himself had shown respect. He had honoured his parents by going back to *"kiss my father and mother good-bye"* when Elijah had initially approached him about becoming his successor (1 Kings 19:20). Then he had consistently honoured Elijah by way of serving him (1 Kings 19:21). He had also been involved with the *"company of the prophets"* listening respectfully to them. As a result they had confirmed his calling as the one who was to take Elijah's place (2 Kings 2:15).

At this point where, literally and figuratively, Elijah's mantle of authority had been placed on Elisha as God's prophet, the aspects of honour and respect were key to the first public miracle that he was enabled to perform. The lack of such respect which then followed resulted in devastating consequences!

First, the positive honouring of Elisha came when he was approached by *"the people of the city"* (2 Kings 2:19). They had an acute problem. Their city, Jericho, was apparently now an up-and-coming attractive location having all the amenities to mark it out as a prosperous and trendy place to live! But there was a problem. It lacked a pure water supply and so the land was *"unproductive".* Agriculture, the livelihood of the inhabitants, was therefore a 'no-go' activity. What was to be done? This was where Elisha came onto the scene, being addressed by those local leaders in a form that honoured his authority and standing even though he was as yet an untested prophet of God: *"Look, our lord..."*

Prompt action

The respect of these leaders was confirmed when they promptly acted on his instructions: *"Bring me a new bowl ... and put salt in it."* This was despite the fact that neither of those actions would seem to have made sense, especially the latter. The nearby Dead Sea, containing a large quantity of salt, was testimony to the fact that *"salt"* did not equate with 'life'! Throwing the salt into the spring from which their water supply flowed, Elisha spoke into the water: *"This is what the LORD says: 'I have healed this water. Never again will it cause death or make the land unproductive'"* (2 Kings 2:21).

A previous curse

The previous inhabitants of Jericho had been at the sharp end of a curse which had arisen many years earlier at the time of Joshua. Israel's leader had pronounced that the rebuilding of that city would result in the deaths of both the firstborn and youngest sons of the man who undertook this task. Elisha now brought the covenant-keeping word of God that spoke life and health into the water, symbolised by the salt (Numbers 18:19, 2 Chronicles 13:5; using the term, *"covenant of salt"*). The outcome was briefly but clearly stated: *"And the water has remained pure to this day, according to the word Elisha had spoken"* (2 Kings 2:22).

The *"people of the city"* had shown respect towards Elisha and they experienced a greater outcome than they may have expected. The 'something more' of God's intervention was of their water supply remaining *"pure to this day."* There is still such a spring in modern-day Jericho called, appropriately, 'Elisha's Fountain'.

Dishonouring ... and its consequences!

In stark contrast Elisha was then approached by a mob of *"youths".* They were young men rather than children, and came from Bethel. They jeered at him with repeated words, *"Get out of here, baldy,"* showing the very opposite of honour (2 Kings 2:23). This phase might have alluded to Elijah being taken up to heaven, and was taunting Elisha to prove his status by having the same experience. Or it could have referred to him going back up to Samaria. But whatever the implication, those youths were on dangerous ground! They were dishonouring Elisha's appearance, age and status. God would be 'touchy' about all three aspects! It was God who had placed Elisha in his role as prophet, and who spoke clearly about respecting those of older years (Proverbs 23:22). Elisha clearly had God's 'stamp of approval' in having spent years alongside Elijah, now bearing his cloak as well as performing miraculous signs that honoured Him.

The insults of those youths towards Elisha resulted in another miracle. But not a positive one! A curse that had been placed on the city of Jericho had been lifted by the power of God's word - now a curse was called down by Elisha, *"in the name of the LORD"* (2 Kings 2:24). As a result, two bears came out of the woods and *"mauled"* 42 of the youths. Although a punishment, this action was not stated to have been fatal, rather it was tempered with mercy. The victims were probably mauled but not killed, like a sharp cuff around the ears, enough to underline the danger of dishonouring God's appointed man (and, by implication, God himself). Better to face a bear on earth, than an angry God in heaven!

Remembering

The two episodes which opened up Elisha's work under God were concluded by the brief verse: *"And he went on to Mount Carmel and from there returned to Samaria"* (2 Kings

2:25). Although no reason was given for this visit, Mount Carmel was recorded as the site where God's power had been evidenced some years previously when Elijah had been prophet. It was here, in answer to prayer, that fire had come down from heaven, vindicating the Lordship of God over all other gods and over His people who had gathered to witness this 'stand-off' between God and the false deity of Baal. It was also here that Elijah had seen God answer earnest prayer, bringing needed rain.

Did Elisha come to that place to remind himself of what God had done in the past and to draw strength from those divine interventions? In one sense such a visit was a way both of respecting the memory and work of Elijah, and of acknowledging God who had brought about those miracles.

Honouring ... and its benefits

In relation to us it should be noted that honouring is initially carried out in the context of the family, and that there is a distinct benefit in doing so. The relevant Commandment reads: *"Honour your father and your mother, so that **you may live long** in the land the LORD your God is giving you"* (Exodus 20:12; emphasis added). This was identified by the apostle Paul as, *"The first commandment with a promise"* (Ephesians 6:2). Moving on from the biological family, this commandment is also to be reflected in the church family: *"The elders who direct the affairs of the church well are worthy of double honour, especially those whose work is preaching and teaching"* (1 Timothy 5:17; also 1 Thessalonians 5:12-13). We are also to honour each other as highlighted by Paul: *"Be devoted to one another ... Honour one another above yourselves"* (Romans 12:10).

Honouring ... God

Finally God is One to whom all glory and honour are clearly due, shown in the reverence and tribute given by the *"twenty-four elders,"* who *"lay their crowns before the throne"* (of God; Revelation 4:10-11). In honouring God and each other we are putting ourselves in a place where we may experience 'something more' from God as He intervenes in our lives.

Reflection

1. In what specific ways can you specifically show honour and respect to those who have some form of authority in your life, such as church leaders, older family members and older / mature Christians? What part can obedience play in this?
2. What difference can there be in showing respect to those in authority whom you know, and those distant from you with whom you have no personal contact (such as those in local or national government)?
3. In what ways are spoken words important in this area of showing honour and respect?
4. What are the ways by which you can specifically demonstrate honour towards God?

Pray: Dear God, You know how this whole concept of respecting and honouring others can be counter-cultural. I need Your help to recognise how I can carry this out in my life.

3. The risk factor

"Whilst the harpist was playing, the hand of the LORD came upon Elisha and he said, 'This is what the LORD says: Make this valley full of ditches. For this is what the LORD says: You will see neither wind nor rain, yet this valley will be filled with water ....'" (2 Kings 3:15-17 NIV 1984)

Read: 2 Kings 3: 1- 25

Smart phones are an essential part of today's 'kit'. To past generations their technology is mind blowing. But they also constitute a 'comfort blanket,' a means of risk avoidance. The chances of getting lost, cut off from other people, left without the ability to pay, and being ignorant of events, are all nullified (mostly). And they satisfy our deepest longing - taking 'selfies'!

But risks are part of life. Some may be reduced but uncertainties and stepping into the unknown cannot be totally eliminated. This is true in our lives as Christians. A relationship with God is not possible without taking risks, moving in faith out of our comfort zones.

An expedition ...

The next account about Elisha experiencing God's intervention sees this element of risk as a key factor. Political instability was the driver of these events involving Elisha. One effect of the disintegration of the original nation of Israel was that the neighbouring kingdom of Moab, previously brought into their sphere of influence by King David, now took advantage of this split and rebelled. King Joram of Israel (the new northern kingdom) consequently planned a military operation in order to bring them back into line.

... and a desperate situation

Somehow the godly King Jehoshaphat of Judah (the newly formed southern kingdom) agreed to be part of this plan. Perhaps he saw a potential danger posed by the growing strength of the rebels and considered Joram less evil than his predecessors. However the tactics for their assault were risky. Their forces not only marched through Judah itself (perhaps another reason for Jehoshaphat's involvement) but also through the country of Edom (whose king added his army to this alliance) before crossing the desert south of Moab. Their attack would thereby be aimed at a less heavily defended area of that country. Whether it was bad planning, poor logistics or sheer incompetence, these attacking forces came to a halt after seven days. They had run out of water, deep in the desert and in a desperate situation.

Up to this point God had been left out of the equation by the kings. The disaster they now faced refocused their perspective. Trouble usually does! Ironically it was the evil king of Israel who first focused their attention on God by way of a question: *"Has the LORD called us three kings together only to deliver us into the hands of Moab?"* (2 Kings 3:10). It was then that King Jehoshaphat pointed to a way ahead by means of a further question: *"Is there no prophet of the LORD here, through whom we may enquire of the LORD?"* An unnamed officer responded with information that Elisha the prophet was in the vicinity. King Jehoshaphat confirmed that *"The word of the LORD is with him."* This was a vital factor in what followed.

A harpist ...

So Elisha was approached by the kings. They initially received a stern rebuke from him. But he then added: *"As surely as the LORD Almighty lives, whom I serve, if I did not have respect for the presence of Jehoshaphat king of Judah, I would not pay any attention to you. But now bring me a harpist"* (2 Kings 3: 14 - 15). Whilst we may feel that characters like Elisha had a 'hot line' to God this was not the case - probably a relief to all of us! In this instance Elisha requested a musician to play a harp. *"While the harpist was playing, the hand of the LORD came on Elisha..."* (verse 15).

The spiritual dynamic of music may not be obvious but Paul hinted at its great value: *"Let the message of Christ dwell among you richly as you teach and admonish one another ....* ***through psalms, hymns, and songs from the Spirit*** *singing to God with gratitude in your hearts..."* (Colossians 3:16; emphasis added). Sung worship can enable us to engage more fully with God as Elisha experienced through the music of the harpist.

... an instruction ...

As God's Spirit came upon Elisha the answer came from God: *"This is what the LORD says: 'Make this valley full of ditches...'"* (2 Kings 3:16 NIV 1984). The kings, in their desperate need of water for their men and livestock, were instructed to dig irrigation ditches in the desert ... with no sign of any water! And nothing happened straightaway: *"For this is what the LORD says: You will see neither wind nor rain, yet this valley will be filled with water, and you, your cattle and your other animals will drink"* (2 Kings 3:17).

... and something more!

But Elisha also brought something more: *"This is an easy thing in the eyes of the LORD..."* (2 Kings 3:18). God spoke not only of the provision of water but also of victory over their enemies. The kings hadn't even mentioned or seemingly thought about this second aspect. But they subsequently achieved victory over the Moabites. Because there was a sequel to the provision, the next morning, of water flowing from the direction of Edom: *"And the land was filled with water."* That same water was seen by the Moabite army as appearing to be blood, with their hasty attack resulting in them being cut down by the Israelite armies.

The risk factor faced by the kings in going along with something that did not seem to be the answer has relevance to us as we encounter situations we cannot control. And God is the One who can still do something more beyond it!

Reflection

1. What makes you averse to taking risks?
2. In what ways do the words in Proverbs 3:5-6 help you to have greater trust in God?
3. What part do God's words play in trusting Him? What has been your experience of hearing God speak as a prelude to trusting Him?
4. What situation involving risk is God using at this time to build up your trust in Him?

Pray: Lord Jesus, please help me 'walk' by faith and not by what I see and understand with my mind and senses.

4. Go with what you've got

"Borrow not a few." (2 Kings 4:3 KJV)

Read: 2 Kings 4:1-7

The word 'miracle' brings up images of dramatic and earth-shattering events taking place in a blaze of publicity. No-one is left unaware of what has occurred. But not all miracles are like that. The previous miracle that God had worked through Elisha in providing water for armies in the desert, then enabling them to achieve victory over their enemies, was witnessed by thousands. But in this next account only four people knew what was taking place.

A crisis ...

It is reassuring to know that God isn't dependent upon awe-struck crowds in order to step in powerfully. A handful of people, a low-key intervention, and a simple act of faith. These are also the ingredients with which He is able to work. The situation leading to this next miracle is particularly low profile. The previous chapter of 2 Kings had seen three heads of state approach Elisha. Now it is just a poor, unnamed, widow who is crying out to the prophet on account of a financial crisis that is seriously threatening her family.

Most of us would more readily associate with this widow than with the kings of 'celebrity' status. Unlike most of those men, however, she comes to Elisha with something of value: a real trust in God. Reference is made to this in her initial approach: *"Your servant my husband is dead, and you know that he revered the LORD"* (2 Kings 4:1). This introduces her as the wife of a man from the company of the prophets, groups that were set up by Samuel, the last judge-leader of the nation of Israel. They were established to train up men in the ways of God and to hear His word in respect of the nation.

... and a question

Somehow this particular member of that company had incurred a debt - perhaps having arisen because of his death - which could only be paid by means of his two sons being taken as slaves. Although there was an element of the Levitical law that provided for people to sell themselves off in this way, they were actually to be treated as hired servants. This would only be for a period, until the Year of Jubilee, when they would be freed (Leviticus 25: 39 - 43; slavery was only to be exercised in respect of those who were non-Jews). Having been informed of this problem Elisha did not tell her that she was in a spiritually bad place, unlike his response to the kings! Instead he faced her crisis with a question: *"What do you have in your house?"* (2 Kings 4:2).

Only *"a little"* ...

When we look for some form of intervention from God we may easily, though subconsciously, reckon on him introducing an outside resource or element; something (or someone) that we haven't got or don't know about. However God's ways of working may often involve the utilisation of something that we already have to hand - to 'go with what we've got'. That was the basis of His question to Moses when confronting him at the burning bush: *"What is that in your hand?"* (Exodus 4:2). The simple response was *"A staff"*. This was probably an old and well-used shepherd's tool-of-trade but was subsequently used by God to miraculously part the Red Sea. David the shepherd had a sling, Shamgar the judge (or 'deliverer') of Israel an ox-goad, and Samson (on one occasion) a dead donkey's jaw bone (see 1 Samuel 17:40; Judges 3:31; 15:15). Each of these objects was unexpectedly used by God to achieve victory over Israel's enemies.

... and *"empty jars"*

So the question that Elisha asks the widow may also be one that God asks us when we come to him with our needs and requests. Our response may also be similar to the widow's ... not a lot! *"Your servant has nothing there at all ... except a small jar of olive oil"* (2 Kings 4:2). It was a similar reply given by another widow some years previously when Elisha's predecessor, Elijah, had approached a non-Jewish widow asking for food. In her case she only had *"a handful of flour in a jar and a little olive oil in a jug"* (1 Kings 17:12). However in both cases it was more than enough when in the hands of God! Elisha instructs the widow to get her neighbours to lend her some empty containers. He emphasises that she is not to ask for just a small number: *"Borrow not a few"* (2 Kings 4:3, KJV). Just as the celebrity-status kings were previously told to dig ditches in anticipation of a supply of needed water, so this widow needed to prepare for God's abundant provision.

Not 'jumping the gun'

But this work of God was to be done in secret. Elisha adds a further instruction following the initial one: *"Then go inside and shut the door behind you and your sons."* God wanted this miracle to be done behind closed doors once the accumulated empty jars were ready. The other containers were then to be filled with the little oil that she possessed. When the last one was full she asked for her son to bring another and, on being informed that there were none left it is stated, *"Then the oil stopped flowing."*

It is interesting that the widow, who now had a houseful of jars filled with oil, did not 'jump the gun.' She did not anticipate what should happen next but reported back to Elisha who, only at that point, told her to sell the oil to pay off the debt and live off the sum that remained. This had only occurred because the woman made what little she had, inadequate as it seemed, available to God. She had experienced God's miraculous intervention in terms of the oil .... then came 'something more' when her sons were saved from slavery.

A staff appointment

A Christian Retreat Centre in the south of England was seeing increased bookings, and so the appointment of a deputy manager was needed in order to share the workload. Use was made of 'networks' and advertising but without any suitable person coming onto the scene. But then it was realised that an existing member of staff - who had initially joined as a breakfast chef - might have the needed qualities for this role. Although having no experience in such a responsible post it was discerned from God that she was the one to be appointed. So someone who was already *"in your hand"* took on this role, the 'something more' element being seen in that she emerged as an excellent manager both in terms of her practical skills and the spiritual qualities that were integral to the job. Do you need to 'go' with what you've already got?

Reflection

1. What can cause us to loose sight of the limited resources and abilities that God has already given us?
2. What is the importance of bringing to God all the resources that we have, recognising that they come from Him and can be used by Him?
3. What can be the reason for keeping a 'low profile' in carrying out what God is telling us to do, as with the widow who poured out the oil away from public gaze?
4. What situation do you face where God may want you to see Him work through seemingly limited resources?

Pray: Heavenly Father, help me see what You have already put into my 'hands' as the means by which You want to intervene in my life.

5. Making space

"Let's make a small room on the roof and put in it a bed and a table, a chair and a lamp for him. Then he can stay there whenever he comes to us." (2 Kings 4:10)

Read: 2 Kings 4:8-37; 8:1-6

Loft extensions are now commonplace but it's not a new idea. Three thousand years ago a *"well to do"* woman in a town called Shunem had similar work done on her property. She particularly wanted it as a facility for the prophet Elisha whom she recognised as a *"holy man of God."* Initially providing him with meals when he was in the area, she arranged with her husband for a room to be constructed on the roof of their house for Elisha *"whenever he comes to us."* The likelihood was that she would have wanted this space for a growing family. But succeeding years had seen this possibility diminish.

Consequences

This woman's openness of heart reached out to the prophet showing warm and practical hospitality. Unexpected consequences resulted from her kindness. She was to experience three successive occasions when God stepped into her life in a way that was outside her expectation.

It is important to see that she played a part in encountering God in these ways. On the face of it there was nothing particularly 'spiritual' about her actions. However the practical steps that she took indicated sensitivity in that aspect of life. She 'sowed' in one area and 'reaped' in another.

1. Seeing a need. Elisha's role as God's representative to the nation was peripatetic in nature. He could not have 'worked from home' even if the technology had been available! Time was spent in various locations where the *"company of the prophets"* were working and studying. He also visited conurbations around Israel such as Dothan and Samaria (2 Kings 6:13, 32). Although it seems that he had his home in the latter he also spent much time 'on the road'.

The woman from Shunem not only identified Elisha's godly character but saw a need for hospitality initially by way of meals ... a good place to start! However this was only part of the 'package'. Having sympathetic company with people on a similar spiritual 'wavelength' and a willingness to spend time with him were also, no doubt, valued by Elisha. Being *"well to do"* she recognised something further could be done. A room on the roof! Was her house the first in town to have an attic conversion? It would have been a clear advance in civilisation!

2. Spending time. The woman's practical action of giving additional help was not a 'flash in the pan'. In one sense her actions to provide meals were in line with the expectations of her culture. It would seem that she had been making such provision for some time. And then a further idea had come to mind. It needed to be discussed with her husband to assess and implement the practicalities involved.

3. Schemng a plan. Having additional accommodation for Elisha was not sufficient. The woman worked out other elements that evolved into a specific plan: *"Let's make a small room on the roof and put in it a bed and a table, a chair and a lamp for him"* (2 Kings 4:10). Her 'down to earth' approach met Elisha's practical needs in carrying out his ministry. He no longer had to worry about booking ahead at a 'Travelodge' or 'Premier Inn'! He could now fully focus on the responsibilities that God had given him.

4. Supplying facilities. Practical steps were taken to implement her plans, and these proved to be effective and appreciated. *"One day when Elisha came, he went up to his room and lay down there..."* (2 Kings 4:11). The woman had stepped out in faith regarding this increased level of hospitality since she was not necessarily certain of Elisha's acceptance of her offer. But what followed, introduced by Elisha 'making himself at home,' showed that he had readily taken up her invitation.

God's first intervention

The first of these interventions arose when he asked the woman: *"Now what can be done for you?"* (2 Kings 4:13). The question was put by Elisha, and he seems to have posed it without any prior warning. It was simply recorded: *"One day when Elisha came ... He said to his servant Gehazi, 'Call the Shunammite.'"* Did Elisha already know the answer that she would give ... and know that it was within God's power to meet her need?

Her reply to the question, and Elisha's suggestion that he obtain some form of official favour from the authorities on her behalf, was that she had no aspirations in that area. Then Elisha's servant stated: *"She has no son, and her husband is old."* Was this her unvoiced response arising from an intense need that she dare not specify?

Now, however, an opportunity unexpectedly opened up for her. It arose in that very place (the extra room) which she may have previously dreamt of as the space she would need for the desired children whom she could not conceive. But God is not ignorant or uncaring in respect of our deep and long-held desires. He is able to intervene at unexpected times and places. For this woman the time seemed to have long passed to have a family on account of her aged husband. Other factors would have compounded her grief. Not only was there social stigma, but she would have felt severe financial and material repercussions on the death of her husband as there was no son to whom family property could be passed to ensure her own support. She could end up desolate and impoverished.

God's favour

In response to his servant's statement Elisha declared to the woman: *"About this time next year, you will hold a son in your arms"* (2 Kings 4:16). Although the woman objected to this with the words, *"No, my lord ... Please, man of God, don't mislead your servant!"* this could be understood as expressing a fear of disappointment rather than a lack of confidence in what was being promised. Faith mixed with doubt. A 'box' that we all 'tick'! Elisha was apparently not put off by this response, and neither was God! We read: *"But the woman became pregnant, and the next year about that same time she gave birth to a son, just as Elisha had told her"* (2 Kings 4:17). Instead of a favour being granted to her in the seat of earthly power she experienced an intervention by God in heaven.

But there was a sequel to this wonderful event. Was it too good to be true? That's what she felt when her young son subsequently succumbed to sickness which affected his head, tragically dying in his mother's arms. She then approached Elisha with the accusation: *"Did I ask you for a son, my lord? ... Didn't I tell you, 'Don't raise my hopes'?"* (2 Kings 4:28). Initially Elisha had been ignorant of the reason for her travelling the distance that she needed to cover in order to confront him in this way. He only identified her *"bitter distress,"* acknowledging that God had hidden the reason for it from him. Clearly Elisha had not expected or received any word from God about this sad event. But he knew that God was not unaware or surprised by it.

God's second intervention

Elisha did not panic but issued instructions to his servant to run ahead of him and lay his staff on the boy's face. Was

Elisha not fit enough to rush to the woman's house where the dead boy had been laid, or did he want to spend time away from the distressing scene in order to pray? His old mentor, Elijah, had previously been used by God to miraculously raise a boy back to life (1 Kings 17:17-24) so perhaps Elisha was reminding God of what He had done in the past. The Bible has many examples of God working powerfully which we can take as encouragements and as a basis for God to do it again!

It is noticeable that the mother had specifically laid her dead son's body on the *"bed of the man of God,"* shutting the door behind (2 Kings 4:21). She was in that room again! It was the place where her dreams had been revealed and God's word of life spoken to her. Although it may not be appropriate to venerate a particular location, remembering places where we have experienced God can be helpful.

Elisha returned to the room on the roof. Although the servant had carried out his master's instructions there had been no change. So Elisha *"shut the door on the two of them"* (his servant and the mother) - who were possibly a negative distraction - and *"prayed to the LORD"* (2 Kings 4:33), a good move! James reminds us: *"Is any one of you in trouble? Let them pray"* (James 4:13). It was after having prayed that Elisha stretched himself over the boy's body which *"grew warm."* He repeated this action. Elisha then paced around the room, perhaps needing to put aside the image of death and focus on God's power as recalled from the past. Then he again laid on the boy: *"The boy sneezed seven times and opened his eyes."* Elisha then summoned the boy's mother. *"When she came, he said, 'Take your son.' She came in, fell at his feet and bowed to the ground. Then she took her son and went out."*

God's third intervention

The woman had one further experience of God's intervention. Having had her dead son restored to life she had then been instructed by Elisha to leave the country on account of a pending famine. Upon return she approached the king for the recovery of her house and land. Unknown to her Elisha's servant had been recounting to the king what the man of God had done. Just as he was describing the woman's son being brought back to life she appeared on the scene to make her request! God intervened in this amazing 'coincidence' to enable her to receive everything back. The king's response to hearing the amazing account of resurrection was to order an official to take up her case and to *"Give back everything that belonged to her, including all the income from her land from the day she left the country until now'"* (2 Kings 8:6). God did 'something more' in a completely unexpected way.

'Something more' was also the outcome in a contemporary setting involving 'space'. A friend and his wife were leading a house church and considering an attic conversion in their home. The hassle and costs were huge factors. But when they met with other church friends God gave a specific direction on this matter - a somewhat cryptic 'God says "yes"' through someone with a prophetic gifting. The resulting additional rooms proved to be of great benefit, spiritually and practically, to subsequent visitors.

Reflection
1. What steps can you take in 'making space' for God to work in your life?
2. What is the importance of timing in responding to opportunities which God may open up?
3. How can the steps taken by the woman (seeing, spending time, planning, supplying) apply to you?
4. What undisclosed dreams do you hold which you need to bring to God?
Pray. Dear Lord, You know the busyness and complexity of life. Grant me the sensitivity to pause and make space for You, and the means by which You want to work in my life.

6. Being real

" ... and there was a famine in that region." (2 Kings 4:38)

Read: 2 Kings 4:38-44

Although the Bible describes people from a very different era, culture and environment to our own, we can readily identify with the feelings and fears of such people. Making poor decisions and having inadequate resources are issues as relevant to our technological age as to that of Old Testament times. So the connected accounts in the life of Elisha recorded in 2 Kings 4 involving bad mistakes and having insufficient resources raise aspects in relation to faith that are applicable to us. They are also relevant to our relationship with God, showing that He can intervene in down-to-earth events even though His methods may be outside our comprehension!

Not exempt

The backdrop to these accounts is that there was a *"famine in that region."* Elisha and the company of the prophets were not exempt from this situation. They, alongside everyone else, were hungry and had run out of food with no means of making anything change. As Christians we too are not excluded from the pressures of life in whatever form they may arise. Unemployment, redundancy, bereavement, illness, dysfunctional family life and cost-of-living concerns are amongst the many stresses that can afflict those who trust in God as well as everyone else. Even though the Promised Land in which Elisha was now living had initially been described as an environment *"flowing with milk and honey"* this was clearly no longer the case. A 'covenant curse' as predicted through Moses had most likely come upon the Israelites because they had deliberately turned from God (Deuteronomy 28:14-24). Even though Elisha and the prophets reverenced and followed God they were still affected by this spiritual fallout. In a similar way the actions and decisions of godless local and national authorities can significantly impact us.

A real-life experience!

In that bleak situation of famine God was able to intervene. But things got worse before they got better! Elisha had given instructions to *"put on the large pot and cook some stew for these men"* (verse 38). So far so good. But then one of the prophets, possibly acting on his own initiative, went out and gathered some unidentified plant cuttings from the fields. They were added to the pot which had probably contained a combination of whatever meagre resources were available. In this case *"no one knew what they were."* But they soon found out! They rendered the stew inedible. As they began to eat they described it as being *"death in the pot"* (verse 40).

Whether this literally constituted a fatal element or was an expression uttered to indicate that the contents were too foul to taste is not explained. But they were very real about their situation. It was not ignored, or labelled in a super-spiritual way, or treated as unimportant. Their plight was obvious, and Elisha did not direct any correction or comment on it as being a trivial issue. Someone's bad but unintentional mistake had severe repercussions ... a very real-life experience!

Further instruction

Although everyone else was helpless in terms of remedying this situation, Elisha knew what to do. He issued a further instruction for some flour to be obtained. This was then put into the container which negated the potent effects of the plant cuttings. He then ordered it to be served with the result that *"...there was nothing harmful in the pot"* (verse

41). This has a parallel with Jesus' miracle of water being turned into wine in that the change only became apparent when it was drawn out of the water jars and served to the master of ceremonies at the wedding (John 2).

Real ... and responsive

Being 'real' is an important element in experiencing God's intervention. Only as we face up to the reality of situations can we fully acknowledge what is happening (or not, as the case may be) and our associated helplessness. Perhaps there may also be a need to face up to our own actions that have led to such problems. The erring member of the company of prophets possibly had to make an embarrassing admission before Elisha was brought into the picture. The approach to Elisha was clearly one undertaken with the realisation that only he, as God's representative, could make a difference in this place of helplessness.

The element of being responsive to God's instruction through Elisha was also important. Adding flour to the contents of the pot may not have made sense. But it needed to be done in order to effect God's intervention and the change that was needed.

When things do not 'add up'

Elisha's servant was also 'real' when subsequently ordered to share out a donation of twenty loaves of barley bread to a large number of people. His response was 'up front' and clearly uttered in desperation: *"How can I set this before a hundred men?"* (verse 43). The figures did not add up as far as he was concerned. We may be in a similar position where things simply do not 'add up.' We may endeavour to trust God in every area of our lives, but then we receive a negative medical report, an upsetting email, a letter of refusal, an exam failure notice, a text message or a knock at the door. These are tangible and real issues that we have to face and cannot mitigate. Elisha was well aware of the real disparity between the number of loaves and those who needed to be fed. But so was God.

"This is what the LORD says..."

As the appointed prophet Elisha was again able to speak the words of God into this situation: *"For this is what the LORD says: 'They will eat and have some left over'"* (verse 43). Having set the food before the crowd it was found that there was sufficient for everyone and that there was actually a surplus as prophesied.

This little-known miracle points to the more widely known one concerning Jesus feeding the five thousand with just five small loaves and two small fish. It underlines the way in which Elisha represented Christ's compassion in an Old Testament environment, and was empowered to speak God's creative word into lives and situations as Jesus subsequently did.

Hot cross buns...

Many centuries later, and across to the east of London, a more recent and similar occurrence involving God's intervention was seen. This was in respect of 'Mill Grove,' the home set up in the early 1900's by Herbert White in Woodford to care for orphaned children. Only this time it was not bread that was featured!

The following extract comes from 'A place for us' (published by Mill Grove, 1976; used with permission). "One of the things Linda and Anne [two of the children who were being looked after in the Home] remember that really helped them to keep going was the incident involving hot cross buns at Easter time one year. Money was scarce and treats were therefore rare between the World Wars. So it was with great excitement that the children and staff looked forward to Good Friday morning with the prospect of hot cross buns for breakfast." As a Christian, and believing that God had directed him to set up this home, Herbert trusted that He would provide all the needed finance and resources. However on this occasion there was no sign of any buns being provided as in previous years.

... a lack of conviction...

“Breakfast was just finishing and the time for prayers had come. Herbert was the last to pray. To all the family’s surprise he ended by thanking God for the hot cross buns. It was faith pure and simple. But had it been misplaced? The family muttered their ‘Amens’, some with a notable lack of conviction. The children in the Home might never know the whole story, but they knew that God had been asked and that the buns hadn’t come. But just as they got up from the large table there was a squeal of brakes outside in the street. Herbert led his own family to the door to discover a van standing right outside. ‘You Mr White?’ the driver enquired. When he was assured that this was the case, he opened the back of the van with the words, ‘’Ot cross buns for you.‘ It was as simple as that as far as he was concerned. All that remained was carrying the trays of buns into the house. That completed, he was off. No one knows who sent him, except that it was not from the usual source.”

... but then more than enough!

This account involving Herbert White even had that ‘surplus’ element as experienced by Elisha and then the disciples of Jesus. They counted over 4000 buns! “And so the children had hot cross buns for breakfast and dinner and tea, even sharing some with neighbours and friends. It was as if God was trying to make the point that supplying the buns for the family wasn’t really that much of a problem as far as He was concerned.”

In each of these accounts the reality of the situation was faced and put to God as an integral step for His intervention ... meaning that it's OK to be 'up front' with Him about our mistakes and needs. Are you?

Reflection

1. What barriers do you need to surmount in order to face up to the reality of adversity and problems confronting you?
2. The accounts in 2 Kings 4 did not record any blame or judgement being passed in relation to the difficulties that had arisen. What is the importance of facing up to the fact that mistakes and misjudgements may be made (resulting in significant problems involving other people) because of human frailty?
3. What is the importance of being specific and open when you bring problems to God, either personally or as a group, especially when others may be affected by such events?
4. Why is it vital to listen to God's response to our prayers for help where they involve action on our part?

Pray: Thank you Heavenly Father that I can be totally honest with You about my mistakes and failings. Help me to be receptive and responsive to Your answers as I look for Your powerful and effective intervention.

7. It's got to go!

"So he went down and dipped himself in the Jordan seven times, as the man of God had told him, and his flesh was restored and became clean like that of a young boy." (2 Kings 5:14)

Read: 2 Kings 5: 1- 27

They desperately wanted to have a family. But despite medical involvement there was no change in their situation. So my friends, committed Christians, made a big decision. Although it was not a practice in their church network, and actually frowned upon in their Christian circles, they took the huge step of seeking prayer in respect of this specific issue. They went outside their denomination and approached an Anglican priest who had a calling from God in praying for healing. My friends had needed to put aside their deeply held theological (and denominational) views to receive prayer in this way. The outcome was God's miraculous intervention. First baby Helen, followed in time by baby Karen!

My friends' action of putting aside their preconceptions of what God could do, and how He should work, was also a necessary step taken by someone else. Naaman, described in the Bible as being in need of God's intervention, came close to missing out because of his own ideas. Rooted in his pride, these had to go before he experienced a miracle.

First impressions

The first impression given of Naaman is of him being the embodiment of maturity. He was the *"commander of the army of the king of Aram* [Syria] *... a great man in the sight of his master and highly regarded."* This was on account of his military achievements and reputation as a *"valiant soldier."* However, whilst his physical ability and bravery were not in doubt he was confronted by another opponent of a completely different nature: *" ... but he had leprosy"* (2 Kings 5:1). It was this physical affliction that revealed the weakness in his character. His faults may not have appeared so crucial in the context of armed combat, but they had to be addressed when it came to the supernatural healing that he needed. However Naaman was resistant to changing his ideas. We are like him in that respect. It is necessary to deal with our preconceptions and underlying pride to enable God to work.

Ready to listen

Naaman had started well. He was ready to listen to the suggestion of a young girl who served his wife. Or perhaps he was simply desperate! The girl, a slave, had been plucked from an Israelite community during one of the skirmishes between the Syrians and the northern kingdom of Israel. Placed in her new family she showed amazing maturity, rising above her hopeless situation by pointing to a source of healing in respect of Naaman's leprosy. She simply stated that there was a prophet in Samaria (Elisha) who, with no 'if's' or 'maybe's,' *"would cure him of his leprosy"* (2 Kings 5:3). The girl's faith was even more remarkable when put alongside her willingness to advance this fact to someone who was not even of the Jewish faith. More amazing was that there had been no previously recorded healing in respect of this condition. If Naaman had 'googled' 'leprosy' and 'healing' then his PC would have come up with the message: 'No matches'!

A political storm

Naaman needed permission to enter what was foreign soil in order to follow through on this girl's information. This showed up the pride in his character that needed sorting out. His high profile status and prestige led him to believe that these were the necessary 'stamps' needed on his 'passport'. Humility was not one of his strong points! Perhaps he had failed to spell out to the king of Syria that it was actually the prophet that he needed to see, rather than the king of Israel to whom he was sent. Armed with a letter to the head of state, plus substantial financial remuneration, Naaman and his entourage headed south ... and into a political storm.

The king of Israel did not respond well to the letter requiring him to *"cure* [Naaman] *of his leprosy."* He took it as a point on which the king of Syria was picking a quarrel with him and he *"tore his robes"*. Whether this was done in anger or frustration was not clear. However the news of the robe-tearing episode reached Elisha who directed that Naaman be sent to him so that *"he will know that there is a prophet in Israel."*

The real problem

The climax to this account was then reached and Naaman's problem was exposed ... and it wasn't his leprosy! The real issue was even more hidden and potent. He, like us, was faced with a choice. Something had to go. It was either his preconceived ideas, arising from his pride, or his disease. Naaman was to find that his need for God's miraculous intervention meant that he had to face up to his real but more deep-seated problem.

Naaman had 'baggage' that needed removing. His surface baggage consisted of *"horses and chariots"* weighed down with ten talents of silver, six thousand shekels of gold and ten sets of clothing. But within himself Naaman had his pride and reliance on possessions which marked his status and worth. They were even heavier than his material wealth now paraded on Elisha's front driveway. What was God's response to this? The account simply states: *"Elisha sent a messenger to say to him: 'Go, wash yourself seven times in the Jordan, and your flesh will be restored and you will be cleansed.'"*

Losing everything

It was possible that this direction from Elisha was greeted with a stunned silence. But then Naaman's emotions went into overdrive. This short message had been delivered, and the front door had then been shut, without any discussion. Naaman went 'ballistic'. *"I thought that he would surely come out to me and stand and call on the name of the LORD his God, wave his hand over the spot and cure me of my leprosy."* He added, perhaps as an afterthought, *"Are not Abana and Pharpar, the rivers of Damascus, better than all the waters of Israel. Couldn't I wash in them and be cleansed?"* Naaman would rather have retained his pride and reputation than lose his lethal leprosy. By doing so he would have lost everything.

The choice that Naaman had to face is one which we may also need to make. Barriers to God's intervention in our lives have to be identified and sorted out. The writer to the Hebrew Christians directs: *" ... let us throw off everything that hinders and the sin that so easily entangles. And let us run with perseverance the race marked out for us"* (Hebrews 12:1).

Others intervene

The account of Naaman shows that God can act even if we are unwilling to face up to our belief that our own ideas, arising from pride, are the only way forward. As Naaman found, it is possible that God will put people alongside us who will assist us in confronting our attitudes! Having performed a skidding reverse U-turn in his chariot (the Biblical account describes him as going off *"in a rage"*) Naaman's servants spoke up. They diplomatically confronted him with two simple facts. First, that if the prophet had required him to undertake some *"great thing"* then he would have done it. Secondly they underlined that he was, actually, only being told to act in a very straightforward way.

These wise observations changed Naaman's attitude. His reaction is described: *"So he went down and dipped himself in the Jordan seven times as the man of God had told him, and his flesh was restored and became clean like that of a young boy"* (2 Kings 5:14). Not only was Naaman's external baggage of horses, chariots and treasure discarded, but so was his clothing. This revealed the full horror and extent of his physical condition. But in doing so he got rid of something else - his pride and reliance on his preconceptions. It was not just one dip in the Jordan that was needed. He was required to go under the water seven times and expose himself to the full view of everyone - a sure way of dispensing with his arrogance and egotism! It was only after that final dip that God's miraculous intervention revealed the outward healing. The Levitical law had prefigured elements of this event. It was prescribed that a live bird was to be dipped seven times into fresh water, and the blood of another slain bird, as a ceremonial cleansing of someone who had recovered from a skin disease (Leviticus 14: 1-7).

Healing...and a sting in the tail

Whilst the root of Naaman's pride had been removed traces still remained. Having returned to Elisha and seen him face-to-face he requested that the prophet receive a *"gift from your servant."* It suggested a reward or payment for this miracle. Possessions were still part of Naaman's make-up. Elisha's response showed that he wanted it publicly affirmed that this miracle came entirely from *"the LORD ... whom I serve."* He would not accept anything. There's no place either for our money or our preconceived ideas to be elements in God's miraculous work.

But there was a sting in the tail. Elisha's servant felt that his master had been too easy on Naaman. So he fabricated a story by which to acquire the gifts that had previously been refused. His subsequent denial of conniving to get hold of this treasure when he was confronted by Elisha resulted in a terrible verdict .... Gehazi had taken Naaman's riches, but he was now afflicted with his leprosy. To his cost this underlined that God's intervention means having to deal with attitudes and ideas. What is it that you need to deal with in this way?

Reflection

1. Why are our preconceived ideas so influential with regard to our view of God and how we think He works?
2. How can our achievements and abilities constitute barriers to us experiencing God's intervention?
3. What is the value of having people bring us a Godly perspective to what is going on in our lives?
4. What actions showing openness to God do you need to take in order to make a way for Him to work in your life.

Pray: Dear God, help me to be open to the ways in which You want to work in my life, putting away *"every weight"* of preconceived ideas and pride within me.

8. The right place

"'Where did it fall?'" (2 Kings 6:6)

Read: 2 Kings 6:1-7

Loss affects us all ... and the need to look in the right place to bring some kind of resolution. It's part of the package of life. Minor irritations like door keys, PIN numbers, appointment letters or any number of items forming part of modern-day 'kit' can easily be lost. However major loss can also be suffered. The Pandemic caused many hopes and dreams to be snatched away, perhaps irretrievably.

Spiritual element

The account of Elisha, and the loss of something, is not only one with which we can identify in a practical way. It also shows God's intervention in a spiritual context, and the importance of looking in the right direction if we are to see Him at work. The details may be different from our own, but the spiritual dynamic behind it is not.

The experience of the *"company of the prophets"* is one which has wider spiritual implications. They were endeavouring to follow God by undertaking a task to facilitate His work. In their case they were looking to extend their accommodation, doing so with the permission and presence of Elisha the prophet of God. But then the unexpected took place. One moment a member of the company was vigorously cutting down a tree for use in the building work, and the next moment the axe-head parted from the handle and *"fell into the water."*

It happened so quickly, and without warning, that preventative action was not possible. It was also an event that was irreversible. The axe-head had last been seen, or heard, creating a splash somewhere in the Jordan River and it seemed that any effort to locate and retrieve it would not be feasible. The subsequent plaintive cry - *"It was borrowed"* - added to the already bad situation. Either there were insufficient tools to go around, or the prophets did not possess any equipment. Being loaned these valuable implements might have been the only means to accomplish the enterprise.

However Elisha facilitated the miraculous intervention of God in this situation. The loss of the borrowed axe-head would likely require some form of repayment, possibly by means of 'pay-back' community-style work, which would have to be undertaken by the individual to the owner as his 'bondman.' The situation was presented to Elisha with the words *"Oh no, my Lord"* (verse 5), which aptly summed up the sense of desperation! Elisha readily responded and asked where the axe-head had fallen (verse 6).

All he could do

So the man *"showed him* [Elisha] *the place."* That was all he could do, perhaps done with a resigned shrug or a dispirited gesture of the hand. It would have summed up his powerlessness and hopelessness. It is the point where every journey has to be routed before we experience God's miraculous intervention. We have to point to the place where our disappointment and loss has been suffered.

There was no stipulation or suggestion as to what Elisha was to do next. We often fail at this point when we bring our needs to God and then advance our ideas as to how and where He should take things forward. Not a good idea! And there was also no comment when Elisha took action to throw a *"stick"* into the water. Although this strange step was presumably undertaken openly it was observed in apparent silence without the expression of any opinion. But this action *"made the iron float"* (verse 6) and it was then retrieved by the (no doubt grateful) member of the company of the prophets.

Where are we looking?

Are we looking in the right 'place' to see where God is working in a spiritually significant way? Reports from Asbury University in Kentucky of powerful manifestations of God's presence emerged in early 2023. What had started as a simple prayer meeting had carried on for another two weeks in this otherwise off-the-map location. It resulted in many Christians flocking to experience God at this unexpected scene of revival. But an even more unlikely place of God being at work was recorded a few months later.....

Leyton Orient football club .... an unlikely place!

"It's not everyday that you get to see a [professional] football team singing a worship song together! Last night Leyton Orient [playing in the English Football League] secured promotion [from League Two to League One] and amidst their celebrations they joined together to sing 'Old Church Basement,' a Christian gospel song by 'Maverickcitymusic' and 'Elevationworship.' What's more important is that there is a core number of Christians in the team who have testified that God has really been moving behind the scenes throughout the season at the club! Games have been won, promotion has been secured and players' lives have been touched by God."

This report from a Christian news source described how the song had been introduced to the team by one of their members, George Moncur, a committed Christian. However it was not only the players who were impacted by this song which featured powerful truths such as, 'When I think of Your goodness and Your love for me ... the joy of my salvation is coming back to me.' The head coach explained, when interviewed by the secular sports media, that when he first heard the music he had not recognised it, commenting that dressing room songs were normally noisy and incomprehensible! As this was different he went to find out more and was confronted by players enthusiastically singing words which 'hit me there' (pointing to his heart).

Many Christians are seriously looking for God to work in clear and life-changing ways, acknowledging that we have 'lost' the sense and impact of His power and presence. Are our expectations only of particular ways and places in which God might answer our prayers? We may be surprised by the dynamic ways (and places) in which God acts ... somewhere in a river ... a stick thrown into the water ... or in the dressing room of professional footballers.

Where do you need to look for spiritually significant intervention to occur in your life?

Reflection

1. Why is it important for us to acknowledge what we are missing (by way of spiritual vitality) as a starting point to experience God's intervention?
2. Why do we need to be open-minded towards the ways (and places) where God may choose to intervene?
3. What are the dangers of having preconceived ideas as to how and where God will work?
4. Consider the different environments where you spend your time. Are these places where God might have plans to intervene and touch people's lives?

Pray: Dear God, please help me to be alert to the unexpected places where You may want to show Your power to change my life and the lives of others.

9. Don't panic!

"What shall we do?" (2 Kings 6:15)

Read: 2 Kings 6: 8-23

'State of Fear.' This is the title of a book written by Laura Dodsworth, a journalist, reflecting on the response of government to the Covid-19 Pandemic. Whilst her observations and conclusions on the Lockdowns are not shared by everyone, the basis of her comments cannot be refuted. People are affected by fear. Whilst some are more impacted than others no-one can escape its influence. It is known that a government advisory body was tasked with setting up the means by which the public were 'nudged' into conforming with regulations put into place to stop the spread of the virus. It is reported that those in authority were surprised by the effectiveness of such action. When able to ease the restrictions there was a reluctance by many people to return to normal, pre-Covid, behaviour. 'Fear' is not easily displaced. It is part of the 'package' of our humanity.

Alarm!

It was fear that gripped Elisha's servant. He had woken up one morning and found that Dothan, the city in which he and the prophet Elisha were living, was surrounded by an army of enemy chariots and horses. His response was of alarm and desperation: *"Oh no, my lord, what shall we do?"*

The events leading up to the servant's reaction originated from Elisha's willingness to listen to God regarding the movement of military forces belonging to Israel's enemy, the Syrians, and to pass on this information to the king of Israel. The latter made use of it to take evasive action. As this kept on happening the king of Syria got suspicious, summoned his army officers, receiving an intelligence update from them identifying Elisha as being the source of Israel's inside information. There was no 'mole' as the king had initially thought. Hence his decision to send forces to Dothan to 'take out' Elisha.

Unperturbed!

In the besieged city the servant's outburst contrasted with Elisha's unperturbed demeanour. The prophet's response identified the fear that had generated the servant's desperate question. *"Don't be afraid,"* Elisha instructed him. This was similar to Jesus' response after He had been asleep in the boat whilst his disciples were panicking on account of the fierce storm that threatened to engulf them. There might be a conflict on the horizon generating fear, but both Elisha and Jesus knew that there was a different and perspective-changing factor to take into account. Panic was not on the agenda! More was going on than could be seen.

In the besieged city Elisha identified how this state of fear was to be changed. *"And Elisha prayed, 'Open his eyes, LORD, so that he may see.'"* This had been preceded by the declaration: *"Those who are with us are more than those that are with them."* Elisha's prayer was answered: *"Then the LORD opened the servant's eyes, and he … saw the hills full of horses and chariots of fire all around Elisha."* God's presence was now revealed by way of angelic beings surrounding and defending them despite the enemy's battalions that were threatening to pounce.

Eyes that are opened

We are only too well aware of pressures, obstacles and threats which exist in our lives as followers of God, both individually and as part of His church. But we need to understand that we are neither alone nor powerless. As the psalmist described it: *"The Lord Almighty is with us; the God of Jacob is our fortress"* (Psalm 46:11). This fact had a direct and miraculous impact on Elisha's situation. He prayed for God to bring blindness (and helplessness) upon the enemy troops thereby neutralising the whole army as they advanced to attack. God acted to remove the sight of the soldiers and they were reduced to impotence. But then the graciousness of God was shown through Elisha who, rather than annihilate them, led them to Samaria (the capital city of Israel) and treated them to a feast, having prayed for their sight to be restored. Such kindness was definitely not laid down in the military manual! This action had an effect on the Syrians because we then read: *"So the bands from Aram* [Syria] *stopped raiding Israel's territory."*

No Benefit payments?

The power and presence of God when fear generating situations arise in our lives is a perspective that we can also experience. Such was the case when I was working in a government department. Payments that were due to be made to members of the public had been posted out as normal. But reports were then received that these had not been delivered. There was a laid-down procedure to be followed in such a situation. But when many more similar calls were received it was clear that the standard procedure would be inadequate. So a decision was made that all enquirers were to be offered the opportunity to call at our office the next day. They would then be able to complete the necessary paperwork and be given replacement cheques straightaway. That was the good news - the bad news was that I was the person required to oversee this operation!

Whilst this problem was not the fault of the department it was realised that not everyone would appreciate this fact! Some would be far from happy and vent their frustration inappropriately. So, like Elisha, prayer was my foremost activity that morning on my way to work! In fact I got to the office early to make practical arrangements and also to go into the waiting area where those needing their payments would gather. I knew that I could pray for God's help in that room before anyone else was around. But then I was prompted to go and stand by the main door, locked at that moment until opening time. In the quietness I felt that it was right to pray that God would be there to calm any 'storm' that might arise from those coming into the office with the intent of causing trouble. As I prayed I felt an unusual (for me!) confidence that God would intervene, which He did. Although the customer service staff and I had to cope with large numbers of people, each of whom had to go through the necessary procedures, there were no serious problems. Some were annoyed but not to a great extent.

Although challenges face us we can have the perspective of knowing God's presence and power. What perspective does God want to bring you when fear, or the threat of it, arises?

Reflection

1. What factors in a crisis generate fear within you?
2. In what ways can fear cause you to be so focused on the crisis that you are unable to have any other perspective?
3. What steps can you take to shift your focus onto God in a crisis?
4. What is the value of knowing God's promises, and that He is with you, when challenges cause you to panic?

Pray: Lord Jesus please open my spiritual 'eyes' to be aware of Your presence, and to Your words that bring perspective when I face trouble.

10. Not finished

"When the body touched Elisha's bones, the man came to life and stood up on his feet." (2 Kings 13:21)

Read: 2 Kings 13:14-21

The last recorded miracle of Elisha took place after he had died and been buried. But God was still able to intervene in an amazing way through the prophet's physical, though decayed, remains. It showed Him able to bring about a resurrection of hope. There is always something more to be experienced from God!

The closing years of Elisha's life are not recorded apart from a meeting on his death bed with the king of Israel. It is reckoned that over four decades had elapsed since his previous public appearance. On that occasion he had been instrumental under God in anointing and appointing a new king and dynastic line in the nation of Israel. It was this new king's grandson, King Jehoash, whom we read of as approaching the dying prophet. There had been continuing turmoil in the nations of Judah (in the south) and Israel (in the north). Most of the kings in these countries had turned away from God (although there had been exceptions). As a result there was an ongoing threat from Syria whose military forces were poised to advance into the territories of God's people as a form of divine discipline.

A prophetic action

It was this continuing tension that had motivated Jehoash to visit Elisha and weep over him. The words that he uttered, *"My father! My father! The chariots and horsemen of Israel"* (2 Kings 13:14) expressed his realisation that Elisha, as God's prophet, was of greater value and power than the country's tangible military resources. Elisha's response to the king's desolation was strange. But it was prophetic. He ordered the king to get a bow and to fire some arrows from the open east window. The prophet's hands were placed over the king's hands as he shot an arrow, whilst Elisha declared: *"The LORD's arrow of victory, the arrow of victory over Aram! ... You will completely destroy the Arameans at Aphek"* (2 Kings 13:17). The specific reference to the east window and to Aphek showed that this symbolic act related to the Syrians who, at that stage, were occupying the trans-Jordan territory to the east and whom a previous king of Israel (Ahab) had defeated at a place called Aphek about 60 years earlier. It showed Jehoash that he was to engage the Syrians in battle, and that God would enable victory to be achieved.

Elisha's anger

But there was more. Elisha then instructed Jehoash to take the remaining arrows and strike the ground. The king did so, but only three times, then he stopped. The interval between the last arrow being struck and Elisha's angry words to him is not stated. It was probably a long enough pause to indicate that the king should have resumed the action. This would explain Elisha's response. The king was either unenthusiastic about encountering the Syrians (which was, as Elisha subsequently confirmed, what hitting the ground with the arrows signified), or was unconvinced as to the power of this prophetic act. However Elisha did not doubt the implication of what had taken place. He told Jehoash, *"You should have struck the ground five or six times; then you would have defeated Aram* [Syria] *and completely destroyed it. But now you will defeat it only three times"* (2 Kings 13:19). That is what happened. The end of this chapter described subsequent events: *"Hazael king of Aram* [Syria] *died, and Ben-Hadad his son succeeded him as king. Then Jehoash ... recaptured from Ben-Hadad ... the towns he had taken in battle from his father Jehoahaz. Three times Jehoash defeated him, and so he recovered the Israelite towns."*

Elisha - not the end

Elisha was now dead and the scene of the interview with King Jehoash had taken place when he was *"suffering from the illness from which he died."* But that was not the end of Elisha's impact. In the dynamic way in which God operates, even the lives of those who are now dead can have an effect on this world. This was the case with Elisha some time after his death. *"Now Moabite raiders used to enter the country every spring. Once while some Israelites were burying a man, suddenly they saw a band of raiders; so they threw the man's body into Elisha's tomb. When the body touched Elisha's bones, the man came to life and stood up on his feet"* (2 Kings 13:20-21).

Clearly Elisha was no longer in a state to hear God speak and be empowered to bring God's life-giving words to others and their situations. His physical body had decomposed to the extent that only the bones were left. However there was no dispute as to the identity of these bones. Whilst we may question the practice of some sections of the church in believing that artefacts and remains of the saints have intrinsic power, sometimes God choses to work sovereignly through unusual means. The early Church was described as experiencing *"extraordinary miracles"* that were worked through the apostle Paul *"so that even handkerchiefs and aprons that had touched him were taken to those who were ill, and their illnesses were cured and the evil spirits left them"* (Acts 19:11-12). People also experienced healing when the shadow of Peter fell on them as he passed by (Acts 5:15).

God's intervention through the dead bones of the prophet Elisha points to the hope that He is able to bring to us. Ezekiel was given a vision of dry bones which then came to life, speaking of the hope that God would bring His people in returning them to their land following exile (Ezekiel 37). We too may look at our circumstances and feel that there's no prospect of change. Things may seem 'dead.' But as with the miracle of life that God worked through Elisha, it can be seen that He is able to step into hopeless situations and bring change in unexpected ways.

A derelict building

There did not seem to be much life left in the old and dilapidated building in east London that had once been a home of the Barclay family (the bankers). The crumbling country house now stood alone. The estate that had once surrounded it had been sold off to developers, and terraced housing for the growing population of 1900's London had been built on it. Yet there was to be one final significant role that this house was to play. It became a training centre for missionaries about to serve overseas, providing basic medical skills for use in areas of the globe where health care was non-existent. Renamed 'Livingstone College,' the number of students who received this training each year gradually declined especially after the First World War. The building was eventually vacated in 1947 and then demolished. But this was not before a student named Paul Brand received his training. His medical studies galvanised him into taking up medicine in a formal way which eventually led him to India and drew him to the plight of leprosy sufferers. He subsequently pioneered transforming surgical techniques which enabled patients to regain the use of their hands, an area of the body particularly afflicted by leprosy. Who could have foreseen that a run-down building on the outskirts of London would prove to be a vital stepping stone in changing the lives of countless numbers of leprosy patients around the globe?

Into what part of your life which is currently 'dead' do you want God bring the hope of 'life'?

Reflection

1. Why is 'hope' so important when you face difficult situations?
2. What is the value of placing your hope in God at such times?
3. What steps can you take to place your hope in God?
4. In what ways is the account of Elisha's bones helpful to you in realising that God can work in 'dead' situations?

Pray: Almighty God I ask you give me greater hope so that especially when I am confronted with difficult scenarios, I can look to You to bring life.

SECTION TWO

God's intervention - signposts

Looking at some of the miracles of Jesus - what they reveal about His power to work in our lives in different ways

11. The mundane matters

"What Jesus did here in Cana of Galilee was the first of the signs through which he revealed his glory." (John 2:11)

Read: John 2:1-11

'Signpost' was the term used by John in his Gospel to explain the purpose of Jesus' miracles. These *"miraculous signs"* (John 2:11 NIV1984; also 4:54; 6:14; 9:16; 11:47) pointed to Jesus as God who *"became flesh and made his dwelling among us"* (1:14). John selected seven 'signposts' to feature in his account of Jesus' work on earth. Five of them, including this one in John 2 where Jesus turned water into wine, were not recorded in the other Gospels.

Low key

Whereas the last of these *"signs"* was conspicuous by the dramatic raising of a dead man named Lazarus (John 11), the first one was marked by something different. It was a low key intervention in a comparatively mundane matter. There was no indication or expectation that anything significant was going to take place when Jesus and His disciples attended a wedding in Cana. The event would have been a common and regular event in the community - obviously special to the couple being married, but otherwise nothing out of the ordinary. The furnishings and items needed as part of this social occasion would also not have attracted any attention. The stone water jars that were to prove integral to the miracle were simply used for ceremonial hand-washing. Even the presence of Jesus may not have generated any comment. Although a rabbi, a teacher with a small group of disciples, His actual identity as God's Son was not widely known; He had performed no miracles up to this point.

Running out of wine

Even the problem that emerged as the wedding meal was taking place may not have been unprecedented. Running out of wine could have been experienced on other occasions. But Mary, the mother of Jesus and possibly having some organisational responsibility for this event, perceived something more in respect of this social disaster. She realised that this matter needed to be brought to Jesus, and directed to Him a simple statement: *"They have no more wine"* (verse 3).

Jesus' response to His mother seemed quite abrupt and disconcerting. His question *"Why do you involve me?"* suggested that this problem was not His concern. His follow up statement, *"My hour has not yet come"* (verse 4), also did not appear to be a positive one. Whilst Mary had no precedent on which to anticipate Jesus' miraculous intervention, she did have 30 years of seeing Him at close quarters and she knew by faith that He was the Son of God. And so when Jesus made the statement about His *"hour"* (or *"time"*) Mary would have realised that this referred to when He would openly reveal His identity as God to everyone around. Although that particular *"hour"* had not yet come, it did not prevent Him intervening in power in a less conspicuous way.

"Draw some out"

This realisation of what Jesus was saying led Mary to instruct the servants who were nearby to *"Do whatever he* [Jesus] *tells you"* (verse 5). Further mundane elements of this account then came into play. Jesus intervened in this ordinary social event by directing that the stone jars be filled with water. They would have held up to 30 gallons each. The servants were then told to draw out some water and present it to the master of the banquet who, upon tasting this water now turned into wine, remarked to the bridegroom upon its fine quality: *"...you have saved the best till now."*

The only people who knew what had happened were the servants, and Jesus' disciples who *"believed in him"* as a consequence of *"the first of the signs through which he revealed his glory"* (verse 11).

An uncertain journey

Mary's recognition that something more can be experienced when 'ordinary' problems arise is a perception that we also need to bring into play. On one occasion in my case this involved petrol rather than water and wine! I needed to drive my car, a 'classic' Morris 1000, to a specialist garage for maintenance work including an inspection of the petrol pump. This piece of equipment is essential in pumping fuel from the tank into the engine. However mine had been proving unreliable. Without the petrol the engine (and the car) would stop...without much warning!

So my journey to the garage, several miles away, was one which had an element of uncertainty as to whether I could complete it without any problem. But, although a mundane matter, I believed that it was something about which I could pray, even though I knew of no previous occasion when God had intervened to ensure that a petrol pump kept on pumping! Encouragement was experienced the previous evening when I had attended the Sunday service at church. One of the songs featured in the time of worship included the words 'You go before me, You're there beside me, and if I wander love will find me.' Although it was more likely that the pump, rather than I, would 'wander,' I took comfort from the general assurance that God brought me through that song that He would be with me!

My prayer was answered in terms of an uneventful drive to the garage the following day. The mechanic's subsequent inspection of the pump was inconclusive as to the cause of its occasional malfunction. But his suggestion that it should be replaced with a new unit was one that I readily took up! God still intervenes in situations which might seem mundane or ordinary. If they matter to us then they matter to Him. What low-key scenario do you need to bring to God?

Reflection

1. What makes you reticent about sharing problems which might appear mundane: with other people, or with God?
2. Are there any indications in John 2 that Jesus was willing to intervene in this situation? How does that encourage you?
3. What does Hebrews 6:12 say to you about how you can approach God whatever the issue which may require His intervention?
4. What steps can you take, learning from the example of Mary, to raise your expectation that God wants to intervene even in mundane matters?

Pray: Heavenly Father, I ask for an increased confidence in You so that I might have a firmer grasp of Your willingness and ability to intervene in the ordinary issues of my life.

12. Trusting ... despite the crisis

"The man took Jesus at his word." (John 4:50)

Read: John 4:46-54

Crisis! This is a word with various connotations, many of them negative, like having fear, being overwhelmed and out of control. It also has the element of being both unavoidable and uninvited, with inevitable adverse outcomes. The recent Pandemic constituted a series of crises for many people which impacted them in different ways - physically, mentally, financially, socially, spiritually.

For the royal official described in John 4 the negative elements of a crisis were very much in evidence. He was faced with the declining health of his son who was *"close to death"* (verse 47). The steps that he took which led to Jesus' miraculous intervention are ones which we can also take when gripped by a crisis.

1. Calling out to Jesus

The father's desperate situation regarding his son caused him to take drastic action. He travelled over hilly terrain by foot, a distance of around 16 miles from his home in Capernaum, to Cana in Galilee. Although having status, 'connections,' and a position of authority in his community, none of these helped him to cope with his son's condition. The helpless and hopeless position which confronted him not only drove him to undertake a difficult day's journey, but he approached Jesus with nothing to offer in return for His intervention. He *"begged him to come and heal his son"* (verse 47). He was calling out to Jesus purely on the basis of the mercy and power which the father believed was part of Jesus' nature.

The Psalmist was someone else who recognised that, in a crisis, God was the only One to whom he could go. *"I cry aloud to the LORD; I lift up my voice to the LORD for mercy ... before him I tell my trouble"* (Psalm 142:1-2). There is a cost in calling out like this. All pretence at our own ability and ingenuity to deal with a crisis has to go. We have to be real with ourselves, and with others, that we are helpless and can only come to God. This was the experience of 33 miners in Chile in 2010, trapped deep underground out of touch with those on the surface following an explosion in the mine's working chamber. But they could call out to God, a step initiated by Jose Henrique, one of the miners, who was a committed Christian. God intervened in this crisis in response to their prayers, enabling contact to be established with the rescuers on the surface, and a bore-hole then engineered through which all the miners were eventually brought to safety in a specially designed capsule.

2. Continued focus on Jesus

The response from Jesus to the official's plea for help did not seem positive. His words did not address the crisis and appeared to constitute a rebuke: *"Unless you people see signs and wonders you will never believe"* (verse 48). However Jesus was actually highlighting a perspective which was intended to encourage trust in Him. Regardless of whether or not *"signs and wonders"* were evident, Jesus was pointing out that He was still One in whom trust could be placed. The father grasped the point. His faith was not based on outward indicators; he continued to focus on Jesus and repeated his request: *"Sir, come down before my child dies"* (verse 49). Persistence in this way, even in the face of seeming (or actual) discouragement, is a consistent factor if we want to experience something more of God's intervention in our lives.

3. Convinced that there is something more

But what marked out the father's response to Jesus was his conviction. Jesus' response to the father's continued plea for intervention was a simple declaration: *"Go ... your son will live"* (verse 50). On the basis of these words alone - no *"signs and wonders"* or any other indicator to back them up - the father *"departed."* He *"took Jesus at his word."* He kept trusting in the words of Jesus throughout his entire journey home, which again took time. It meant that only on the following day did he find that his son had recovered. His servants met him with the news, and he asked when the recovery had taken place. Upon being told that it was *"one in the afternoon"* of the previous day, the father realised that it was the exact time that Jesus had made the declaration of healing. This realisation resulted in the official and his whole household putting their trust in Jesus (verse 53).

No money in the bank

In recent times a small group of Christians, involved in printing and posting out evangelical and Bible teaching material overseas, also needed to take Jesus *"at his word."* The 'Gospel Printing Mission' had operated out of a church hall in east London and had annually produced around one million pieces of literature. But it was a low profile operation, with no advertising or canvassing for funds. It was believed that God had said that He would provide the needed finance in response to prayer. So on this basis an order was placed on one occasion for a further supply of paper even though there was a crisis: no money was in the bank account to pay for it! Even after the paper was delivered and an invoice received, there were still insufficient funds to meet the cost of the material. However a cheque was posted to the supplier, trusting that God would work to provide the money. Unknown to the GPM team various unsolicited and voluntary donations were on their way to the Mission which enabled sufficient funds to be in the account when the cheque was actually presented.

In what situation does Jesus want you to take Him *"at his word"*?

Reflection

1. In what ways does the account in John 4 show you the importance of listening to what Jesus is saying in a crisis?
2. What elements of a crisis drive you to focus on Jesus and to listen to Him?
3. Why is it important that trust in Jesus is not solely based on the *"signs and wonders"* that He can cause to happen?
4. The father was not aware of his son's recovery until the day after he had talked to Jesus. What does this say to you about the time element of Jesus' miraculous intervention in your life?

Pray: Lord Jesus, please sharpen my sensitivity to Your voice so that I can be like the father who took You at Your word.

13. No time limit

"When Jesus saw him lying there and learned that he had been in this condition for a long time, he asked him, 'Do you want to get well?'" (John 5:6)

Read: John 5:1-15

The vastness of outer space means that the distances of galaxies far from our Earth are not measured in miles or kilometres. Astronomers cite distances by way of 'light years.' Light particles travel at the speed of 186,000 miles per second. Using this method with reference to Proxima Centauri, which is our nearest star apart from the sun, it is 4.15 'light years' away. This means that if you could travel at the speed of light then it would take over four years to get there. Being described in this way also saves a great many zeros as compared to writing it out using linear units!

Ongoing discoveries about the universe (the furthest galaxy is an amazing 13.5 billion 'light years' away) give us a glimpse of God's power which extends in ways we cannot grasp. For instance, our concept of 'time' is that it is ongoing and outside of our control. However, whilst we carry on with life within time's constraints - we cannot stop, slow down, speed up, or step out of it - the Bible describes God as working outside of its restrictions. He is eternal and exists outside of 'time.' Jesus, God Who became Man, is described in the context of 'time' as being the *"Alpha and Omega ... who is, and who was, and who is to come ... the First and the Last.."* (Revelation 1:8, 17).

1. Scheduled meeting

Yet Jesus stepped down into 'time,' and its restraints, to live in this world. And His intervention in the lives of those around Him showed, sometimes in very clear ways, that His control of what was taking place included the 'time' factor.

This was integral to the miracle relating to the man by the Pool of Bethesda. The scene in John 5 is immediately set with reference to 'time' which points to Jesus' control in that element: *"**Sometime later**, Jesus went up to Jerusalem for one of the Jewish festivals"* (verse 1; emphasis added). Jesus was undertaking a specific journey at a particular time. Nothing that Jesus undertook during His ministry was by chance, unplanned, co-incidental, haphazard or done on the spur-of-the-moment. Jesus was always conscious of the importance of doing things at the right time. He was also committed to doing *"the will of him who sent me and to finish his work"* (John 4:34). Prior to this journey to Jerusalem Jesus had met a woman by a well. The account records that He *"had to go through Samaria"* for that purpose and specified the time, *"about noon"* (John 4:4,6) which pointed to this as a planned encounter with someone who had a deep spiritual need.

To Ponder: Relationship with Jesus involves trusting Him about the schedules and plans that He has for us, about which we may not be aware until they come into play.

2. Stepping in

Jesus' visit to Jerusalem led Him to a pool called Bethesda. It was here that He stepped into an environment where the ravages of time were particularly evident. *"Here a great number of disabled people used to lie - the blind, the lame, the paralysed"* (verse 3). These conditions, by their very nature, would have deteriorated or given rise to other disabilities as time progressed. The limited knowledge in medical science, and general neglect that would have existed in those days, would have compounded the plight of those at Bethesda. The name meant 'House of mercy' and is perhaps connected with the description (included in some less reliable documents pertaining to John 5) of angelic visitations being experienced from time to time whereby the water in the Pool was disturbed. The person who then entered the water first following this event was said to be healed of their condition.

However Jesus had not gone to Bethesda simply to observe the invalids and their vulnerable state. The account implies that Jesus looked for the person who had been sick for the longest period of time, that is, the worse case scenario. *"When Jesus saw him lying there and learned that he had been in this condition* ***for a long time...*** *"* (verse 6; emphasis added). 'Time' had significantly impacted this man, who had been disabled for 38 years.

Jesus' intervention in the life of someone marked out by the longevity of their illness is also recorded on other occasions. A woman suffering from bleeding for 12 years (Luke 8), a woman crippled for 18 years (Luke 13), a man who had been mute since a child (Mark 9), and a man born blind (John 9), were others for whom the duration of illness was no barrier to the healing that Jesus brought to them.

In response to Jesus' question, *"Do you want to get well?"* the man at Bethesda replied that he had no-one to help him to get into the Pool following the supernatural stirring. 'Time' was again a factor in his life. Someone else was always quicker than him. The tone of anguish could be sensed in this response, something which can easily develop as situations are viewed as beyond hope, and with no prospect of change as time goes on. But Jesus wanted to show this man that with Him it is never too late.

To Ponder: The work of Jesus in our lives is not governed or determined by the passing of time alone.

3. Sudden change

This man's condition that had afflicted him for years, with no hope of any improvement, was suddenly changed! Jesus spoke words into his life: *"Get up! Pick up your mat and walk"* (verse 8). The element of 'time' was particularly evident in what happened next. *"**At once** the man was cured; he picked up his mat and walked"* (verse 9; emphasis added).

Jesus' words had power to bring immediate change, as had also been clearly shown on other occasions. *"Be clean"* (Mark 1:41; to a man suffering from leprosy), *"..rebuked the fever"* (Luke 4:39; to Peter's mother-in-law), *"Come out of this man"* (Mark 5:8; addressed to the demons oppressing a man), *"Stretch out your hand"* (Mark 3:5; to the man with the withered arm), *"Quiet! Be still"* (Mark 4:39; addressed to the forces of nature threatening to overwhelm the boat in which Jesus and His disciples were sailing), *"My child, get up"* (Luke 8:54; to the young girl who had died). In each of these cases, and with no discernible delay, Jesus' words brought change and deliverance into the lives and circumstances of those to whom He spoke where the 'time' factor was also prominent. Jesus stated that His words were *"full of the Spirit and life"* (John 6:63).

To Ponder: Jesus' work and intervention in our lives may involve a process which takes time. But we need to be open to the possibility that sometimes He may effect change with no delay.

4. 'Sabbath-day syndrome'

After this miraculous healing the 'time' factor surfaced in another way. The Jewish religious leaders saw the man carrying his mat and pointed out that, as it was the Sabbath day, he was doing something that the Law prohibited. However Jesus, having clearly told the man to pick up and carry his mat - evidence of the healing power that He had brought to him - had a different perspective. He highlighted His deity, and His authority to act in the timing that He ordained, when He stated in response to them: *"My Father is always at his work* ***to this very day,*** *and I too am working"* (John 5:17; emphasis added).

The 'Sabbath-day syndrome' can still be seen in our own age when our preconceived ideas about when God should be expected to intervene may affect our perception. One of the miracles recorded in connection with the Early Church involved a crippled man to whom God brought healing through Peter and John. The conclusion of this account, which again involved the religious leaders raising the issue of performing a healing on the Sabbath day, recorded a further element: *"...all the people were praising God for what had happened. For the man who was miraculously healed was* ***over forty years old"*** (Acts 4:21-22; emphasis added). His age and condition are particularly noted. The inference is that someone of his age could not expect to experience such a change at his time of life.

Time dragging on

When a situation has dragged on for a long period and the age of the person involved is clocking up, the expectation of Jesus' intervention can come under strain. But in that context a Christian writer brought this encouragement: 'Don't believe your dream is dead and will never be fulfilled. And don't believe those who tell you that you're too old to fulfil the dream God gave you. God can pack more into the last chapters of your life than all those that precede them' ('Word for Today,' Bob Gass - United Christian Broadcasters).

The experience of a member of a small church on the borders of London and Essex showed how Jesus could enable change to be experienced when experts deemed that it was too late, or someone was too old, for anything to change. Eric, in his late 80's, suffered a fall at home and broke his back. He was in hospital for many weeks and the medical team pronounced that he would never be able to walk again. However his resolute Christian faith, and his desire to provide care for his sick wife, resulted in him regaining his mobility, walking with the use of aids, despite his advanced years and the medical prognosis.

The man at the Pool of Bethesda had, most likely, woken up that morning with the expectation that the day ahead of him would be the same as each previous day for the past 38 years. But Jesus' miraculous intervention meant that he went to bed that night with a life that was changed beyond anything he could have imagined 24 hours earlier.

To Ponder: Jesus does not have 'sell-by' dates (as we understand them) which determine the point beyond which He cannot intervene to bring change into our lives.

Reflection

1. What steps can you take to be more aware of the timing of God's work, and what He wants to do, in your life?
2. What encouragement can you draw from knowing that Jesus is aware of all the adverse situations you face, and is able to 'step into' those that are long-standing?
3. What does Jesus' instruction to the man at the Pool (and the other examples mentioned above) show you about the power of His words to bring transformation?
4. In what ways does the account of Zechariah and Elizabeth becoming parents despite their advanced years reinforce God's ability to work outside of preconceived ideas regarding 'time' (Luke 1:5-23)?

Pray: Dear Jesus, please change my expectations about 'time,' and open to me to Your ability to intervene outside of its constraints which affect me.

14. Out of control

"...for He already had in mind what He was going to do." (John 6:6)

Read: John 6:1-13

The iconic and long-running television science fiction series, 'Dr Who,' has often seen the Doctor matched against his arch-enemy, the Daleks. These robotic-type creatures, wielding their death rays accompanied by the fear-inducing words 'Exterminate! Exterminate!' have caused many younger viewers to hide behind the sofa! But the Doctor always finds a way of neutralising their plans for domination and on one occasion his intervention caused a posse of Daleks to move around erratically uttering the cry 'Out of control! Out of control!'

Those words may echo the feelings that we have when crises arise, bringing with them a sense of helplessness and hopelessness. But this response is not limited to us. The miracle of Jesus feeding five thousand men (plus women and children) with five *"small"* loaves and two *"small"* fish (John 6:9) showed His intervention in a scenario where people were not in control. This account is relevant to us, who live in times when information technologies and media sources only serve to highlight how little we are in control of our circumstances.

'Throwaway' comment

The feeding of the five thousand clearly impacted the Gospel writers because it is the only miracle that they all include in their narratives. However it was John alone who described the conversation that took place between Jesus and Philip, His disciple, where the almost 'throwaway' comment was made: *"He asked this only to test him,* ***for He***

already had in mind what He was going to do *"* (verse 6; emphasis added). This had followed Jesus' question about where bread could be bought for all *"these people to eat."* Jesus was aware of what was happening, and was in control of the situation as shown by His miraculous intervention. However this was not only in respect of the actual provision that took place, but in other ways that are also relevant to us.

1. *"He already had in mind ...."* - Change

Matthew's account sets the scene for this miracle. He describes Jesus' response to the terrible news of John the Baptist's execution that had been ordered by King Herod. John, outspoken against the king's immorality, was Jesus' cousin and his death caused Jesus to seek solitude: *"He withdrew by boat privately to a solitary place"* (Matthew 14:13). Mark's account brings a further factor into this decision to find a place for reflection. The busyness that the disciples were experiencing resulted in His direction: *"Come with me to a quiet place and get some rest"* (Mark 6:31-32). So Jesus and His disciples got into a boat to cross the Sea of Galilee, a large lake about 13 miles long.

However their movement had not gone unnoticed. *"But many who saw them leaving recognised them and ran on foot from all the towns and got there ahead of them"* (Mark 6:33). So, instead of a location where there was serenity, peace and quiet, Jesus arrived to find His destination crowded with people! This was a big change to what might have been expected. John's account reveals the motivation for the journey that all these people had undertaken: *"...because they saw the signs he performed by healing those who were ill"* (John 6:2).

Jesus' response

What was Jesus' response to this change to the planned quiet retreat? Mark described His reaction: *"When Jesus landed and saw a large crowd, he had compassion on them, because they were like sheep without a shepherd. So he begin teaching them many things"* (Mark 6:34). Matthew adds: *"... He had compassion on them and healed their sick"* (14:14), whilst Luke records that Jesus actually *"welcomed"* all these people (Luke 9:11)!

'Change Management'

The unpredictability of events in life can arise suddenly and affect us deeply. We can find ourselves thrown into panic and confusion by situations that unexpectedly change. Whilst there may be actions we can take to mitigate the effects of unforeseen circumstances the impact can still be devastating. Whilst working in a civil service department I was sent on a course entitled 'Managing Change' designed to help staff cope with the constant flow of instructions and directives amending work processes. Those of us who had been in the department for some time felt that this course served another purpose - handling the fallout from inadequate and inept planning by senior management!

But whatever the cause of an unexpected change, the account of the feeding of the five thousand can bring us assurance. Jesus is not fazed by change. He brought healing, insight and compassion to people in the changing situation that emerged. He *"already knew what He would do"* when others were confused. Now He can come to us, able and willing to release His life-giving power and insight when we face sudden and substantial changes.

2. *"He already had in mind .... "* - Crisis

The second aspect of this miracle that emerges is the timing integral to unfolding events. As Jesus looked at the people and intervened in their lives with compassion, His disciples started to look at their watches, or the equivalent! Each of the Gospel writers specifically refer to the time element linked to the looming crisis as they saw it. *"As*

evening approached*, the disciples came to Him and said, 'This is a remote place, and it's already* ***getting late.*** *Send the crowds away, so that they can go to the villages and buy themselves some food'"* (Matthew 14:15). *"'This is a remote place,' they said, 'and it's* ***already very late****…'"* (Mark 6:35). *"****Late in the afternoon*** *the twelve came to Him and said, 'Send the crowd away…'"* adding, *"'…and find food* ***and lodging****'"* (Luke 9:12; all emphases added).

The 'ticking' clock

The situation highlighted by these verses is also relevant to us. Problems arise but there is no time to resolve them or it's too late to get help. 'Deadlines' cannot be pushed back and limited resources cannot be supplemented within the set time. However, even with the clock 'ticking', Jesus is not overwhelmed by the approaching crisis and associated time factor.

The Gospel writers record Jesus directing His disciples: *"You give them something to eat"* (Matthew 14:16; Mark 6:37; Luke 9:13) with John's narrative bringing His question to Phillip: *"Where shall we buy bread for these people to eat?"* It was this enquiry that introduced the statement that Jesus already had in mind what He was going to do. However Andrew's appearance onto the scene at that point did not seem to provide a solution. The boy's provision was notably inadequate: *"…five small barley loaves, and two small fish."* Hence Andrew's question: *"…but how far will they go among so many?"* Jesus, however, viewed this as God's provision that had already been put in place to meet the crisis.

The fact that Jesus already knew what lay ahead, and what He was able to do about it, totally removed both the crisis itself and the pressure of time. Jesus' power and knowledge have not subsequently diminished or become variable. He is the same *"yesterday and today and for ever"*

(Hebrews 13:8). Even when we are overwhelmed by challenges where time is an integral element He is still able to intervene.

Eddie Stobart

When Eddie Stobart, a committed Christian and founder of the logistics-distribution business, started out in the transport industry his initial and sole contract was to haul fertiliser to local farmers in his area of Northwest England. But he was suddenly notified that the contract would be terminated at the end of the month. The clock was 'ticking' and the livelihood of Eddie, and his employees, was under serious threat.

However he believed that God could intervene. Without having been specifically proactive, he was unexpectedly approached by a local manufacturer who needed extra transport capacity and asked for his help. The distribution of tin cans which arose from this contact proved to be the catalyst to Eddie's name becoming synonymous with road haulage. God knew before the crisis both what was needed and when to provide it. He can do that for you too.

3. *"He already had in mind .... "* - Confusion

The miraculous feeding also showed that, having in mind what He would do, Jesus' actions addressed potential confusion. This is an aspect of events that seems to have escaped much attention. But organising the distribution of food to such a large crowd without the aid of 'WhatsApp' would not have been straightforward! Jesus gave specific instructions as to what was to be done: [1] *"Make the people sit down."* [2] *"Jesus then took the loaves, gave thanks..."* [3] *"...and distributed to those who were seated"* (by way of the disciples handing out the food); [4] *"He did the same with the fish."* [5] *"...he* [then] *said to his disciples, 'Gather the pieces that are left over...'"* (John 6:10-12).

The step-by-step instruction that took place prevented any confusion either on the part of the crowd or His disciples. This approach is also vital when we receive direction in our own lives. Whilst we may want to know exactly what is going to happen, how things will turn out and when, Jesus often simply speaks to us about the next step, as distinct from the next half dozen! We may not feel comfortable with this methodology! But it means that we develop trust in Him and it keeps us focused. In terms of the way ahead He 'already has in mind' the path ahead of us.

God always has 'something more' for those who are committed to Him, even when we are confronted by change, crisis and confusion. Whilst these may throw you off balance, do you remind yourself that He is the One who 'already has in mind what He is going to do'?

Reflection

1. What are the aspects of sudden change that can particularly impact you, and what initial steps can you take (arising from a relationship with God) to prevent 'meltdown'?
2. Why is 'time' such a pressing factor, and what does Jesus' calmness in the face of the clock 'ticking' reveal to you?
3. In the light of Jesus' response to this situation, what measures can you take to prevent confusion from dominating your life, particularly when you face challenges?
4. What does Jesus' action to avoid potential confusion prior to actually performing the miraculous feeding teach you about the value of order and thinking ahead?

Pray: Lord Jesus, You know how life seems to throw so many challenges in my direction. Thank You that You know all about such things. I ask for Your help to keep focused on You.

15. Nothing to go on

"When they had rowed about three or four miles, they saw Jesus approaching the boat, walking on the water; and they were frightened." (John 6:19)

Read: John 6:16-21

Google and other internet search engines seemingly provide us with a ready source of limitless information. We have an expectation that current technologies mean that we are never left with unanswered questions or gaps in our knowledge. So should Google respond to an enquiry in a negative way it can cause us surprise and concern!

The disciples of Jesus may have thought that they knew all about their environment. Most of them had probably been around the Sea of Galilee since birth, certainly some of them were experienced fishermen. But when they saw Jesus walking on the water towards the boat they were rowing, it was an event completely outside their expectation. Had they googled 'Walking on water' it would have responded with 'No match' in big bold letters! There was no precedent for what they were witnessing. Nothing like it had previously been recorded in the Bible, and it proved to be an unrepeated event. The disciples had nothing to go on. Their response of being *"frightened"* is probably an understatement!

However this account of Jesus walking on water, although without precedent, highlights aspects of His miraculous interventions which are relevant to His potential work in our lives.

1. Surprising

The parallel account in Matthew 14 gives the background to this miraculous walk. Jesus had performed the miracle of feeding a crowd of five thousand people gathered in a remote place with just five loaves and two fishes. He had then instructed His disciples to get into a boat and return ahead of Him to the other side of the Sea of Galilee. Whilst they were rowing across to a town called Capernaum Jesus went up a mountain to pray. Meanwhile the disciples encounter rough and adverse conditions affecting their voyage. Mark records: *"He* [Jesus] *saw the disciples straining at the oars, because the wind was against them"* (Mark 6:48). And so, with the disciples having rowed for much of the night and still only reaching around the halfway point *"Shortly before dawn Jesus went out to them, walking on the lake"* (Matthew 14:25).

What needs to be stressed is that this action of Jesus is not only unprecedented, but also unannounced. He had not previously informed His disciples that He was going to meet them in this way, it was not on any weekly schedule that had been issued to them, and it was not included in an action plan that had been drawn up. It was a complete surprise and totally unexpected.

Jesus' intervention in our own lives may, in a similar way, be both unannounced and surprising. Whilst we like to know what is happening - and current worldviews suggest that we have the right to know in advance what is going on - His actions are not bound by what we want or expect! But that can also result in us questioning whether He is able to work in situations where His miraculous intervention may not (to our knowledge) have been previously exercised. Some time ago I was involved in a local church where, as a means of involving youngsters in the life of the church, we held Saturday lunchtime mini-football tournaments on the nearby college astroturf pitch. However these had to be stopped because the pitch was deteriorating and unsafe to use. Although the college provided an alternative asphalt surface this was not ideal; they were also not forthcoming about any plans to provide a new astroturf. However we believed that we could pray to God to sort out this situation ... by somehow providing a new pitch. But we realised that there was no precedent for this request. Did God know anything about astroturf pitches? Had He ever been previously presented with such a situation? Acting on God's prompting, we actually prayed for Him to intervene whilst we stood by the old astroturf surface one Saturday lunchtime in front of the youngsters (including local lads who had joined us by this time). To our surprise, and without the college telling us, we saw work start the following week, mechanical diggers ripping up the old surface to prepare for a new pitch!

To ponder: Jesus can intervene in situations and ways that may completely surprise us.

2. Sudden

A further feature of this miracle is the timing. Jesus walks on water *"shortly before dawn"* (Matthew 14:25; Mark 6:48); *"...it was dark"* (John 6:17). The disciples are not anticipating that at this point they will encounter Jesus in this way. They have no text alert to inform them that something is going to happen, nor is it a previously arranged appointment. Our own culture is geared to providing the fullest possible information about the timing of events. There seems to be an app for everything in order to keep us 'in the loop.' But God is under no such obligation, and sometimes works when we least expect it.

But a further element of timing is also present in this miracle. Both Matthew and Mark record an immediate change that takes place: *"And when they* [Jesus and Peter] *climbed into the boat, the wind died down"* (Matthew 14:32); *"Then he* [Jesus] *climbed into the boat with them, and the wind died down"* (Mark 6:51). The wind that had been adversely affecting the disciples' progress up to that point ceases to blow a gale as soon as Jesus (and Peter, whose venture onto the water is only recorded by Matthew) steps into the vessel. John's account describes an even greater change that took place. *"Then they* [the disciples] *were willing to take him* [Jesus] *into the boat, and* ***immediately the boat reached the shore*** *where they were heading"* (John 6:21; emphasis added). Having battled against the elements for almost the entire night in an attempt to row to the other side of the lake, as soon as Jesus joins them the disciples' boat is at its desired destination! This is almost in the realms of 'Star Trek' and 'Beam me up Scotty'! It's a reminder that God is not restricted by time. He declares: *"I am the LORD; in its time I will do this swiftly"* (Isaiah 60:22).

A friend and I regularly spent time together talking and praying through different issues that we were facing. During the Pandemic, having recently left his job in Christian work, he was particularly looking for a further way to serve God. In that time of lockdowns and furloughs such a prospect looked unlikely. But God suddenly and unexpectedly intervened to change my friend's situation. He was invited, without any convoluted processes, and out of the blue, to take on the leadership role of a small church on the Essex border, something he readily accepted.

To ponder: Jesus can intervene at a time that we do not anticipate...and work quicker than we expect.

3. Spooky

A third aspect of Jesus walking on water is that it was spooky, and something completely outside of the disciples' experience and terms of reference. They are completely unable to understand what is happening. *"When the disciples saw him* [Jesus] *walking on the lake, they were terrified. 'It's a ghost,' they said, and cried out in fear"* (Matthew 14:26). This reaction necessitates Jesus having to calm them down: *"Take courage! It is I. Don't be afraid"* (Matthew 14:27). Whilst the description 'spooky' (alongside 'freaked out') is not used in the Bible, this contemporary term encapsulates the disciples' response!

Understanding situations we face may give us a sense of being in control even though we may not be able to change them. The response of the disciples was generated both by a lack of understanding and an awareness of being out of control. But again God is not restricted to working in ways that we can understand or follow. Whilst His intervention may not be so awesome as that experienced by the disciples, He may chose to act in ways that leave us speechless. Whilst attending a Bible summer conference some time ago I was walking back to the car park from the camping area. Unexpectedly, and on a site of several thousand attendees, I suddenly passed someone I recognised from the past. We spotted each other simultaneously, each of us having an expression on our face as if to ask 'What are you doing here?' We had previously known each other from a church where he had been engaged in leadership training. But he had moved on and we had lost contact until that moment at Shepton Mallet. That unanticipated meeting proved to be instrumental in subsequently opening up the opportunity for me to provide input into his church.

To ponder: Jesus may chose to intervene in challenging situations in ways outside of our terms of reference.

4. Specific

Lastly this miracle shows Jesus' intervention directed to the lives of specific people. Whereas the previous miracle involved feeding five thousand people, when He walks on water He appears only to the twelve disciples. And, as we have seen, these men are not in a good spiritual state. They are *"frightened..terrified..cried out in fear"* and need assurance from Jesus to calm them down. Peter, who asks Jesus to bring confirmation as to His identity by inviting him to walk on water, is distracted by the wind. When Jesus reaches out His hand to catch him it is an action accompanied by the words: *"You of* ***little faith****...why did you doubt?"* (Matthew 14:31; emphasis added). But at least Peter has stepped out of the boat. The eleven others remain on board, raising the question as to their level of faith compared to Peter's! Mark adds a postscript regarding their spiritual state: *"They were completely amazed, for they had not understood about the loaves;* ***their hearts were hardened"*** (Mark 6:52; emphasis added). This attitude of the disciples reassures us that we may experience God's intervention whatever the level of our spiritual sensitivity. In His mercy and kindness He may still work even though we may have 'lost the plot' or not have a clue.

There is one other factor that should be taken into account. Max Lucado, an American author, has written many books about Christian living. One of them is entitled 'He still moves stones.' This refers to God removing the stone from the tomb to enable people to see that Jesus had risen from the dead. In the context of this account in John 6, that title could also read 'He still walks on water.' But Lucida's book also has a subtitle: 'Everybody needs a miracle.' It is a reminder of God's ongoing ability and willingness to step into our lives, even when we have 'nothing to go on.'

To ponder: In what area of your life do you need to recognise that Jesus is able and wanting to work?

Reflection

1. Why may not having, or knowing about, any precedent be an obstacle when you pray to God about an issue?
2. How can you generate a more open-minded approach to the ways (and timings) in which God may choose to intervene in your circumstances?
3. What barriers do you feel exist that prevent you from experiencing God's intervention in a personal way?
4. What steps can you take to remove these barriers?

Pray. Thank you Lord Jesus that You still 'walk on water,' whatever stormy and unprecedented issues I may face.

16. Probing questions

"He replied, 'The man they call Jesus made some mud and put it on my eyes. He told me to go to Siloam and wash. So I went and washed, and then I could see.'" (John 9:11)

Read: John 9:1-41

Did Neil Armstrong really walk on the moon's surface in 1969? Was the shot by Geoff Hurst in the 1966 Wembley World Cup Final fully over the goal-line? And was Christopher Columbus actually the first European to discover the New World in 1492?

Exploits that capture the headlines often generate scrutiny and questions. Authenticity is at stake. So in that light Jesus' provision of sight to a man born blind did not go unnoticed. A barrage of questions and possibilities had arisen from this extraordinary miracle. Not only had Jesus given sight to someone who had never been able to see, but this intervention had taken place on the Sabbath day. It would seem that Jesus had gone out of His way to draw people's attention to what He had done. It meant there was really no option for people to 'sit on the fence.'

Raising questions

The miraculous intervention of Jesus in people's lives today, even in low key issues, continues to raise questions and present difficult issues which need to be addressed at a personal level. Christians differ in their beliefs whether miracles should still be expected. So this incident in John 9, and the fallout that it created, is still relevant to us.

The first question is raised by the healed man's neighbours and those who had previously seen him begging: *"Isn't this the same man who used to sit and beg?"* (verse 8). It immediately reveals divided opinions: *"Some claimed that he was. Others said, 'No, he only looks like him.'"* This particular group of people would have known the man very well as he was a familiar figure who sat begging all day. The doubt that arose in the minds of some people concerning his identity could have arisen because they had not looked hard enough to see that he was the former beggar. The miraculous work of Jesus today can be missed simply because of our lack of attention, especially in what may be termed the undramatic interventions we may experience. The pace and pressures of life can prevent awareness of God being at work. Are we alert to God's intervention in less dramatic ways?

Demanding

The second question follows from the first. Having satisfied themselves that it is the beggar who can now see they demand: *"How then were your eyes opened?"* John uses the word *"demanded"* (verse 10, NIV 1984). It suggests that they are looking for information by which to verify what had taken place. But the man's reply, an explanation that he was to repeat to the religious leaders, leaves no room for any other conclusion but that a miracle must have been performed. In our contemporary scene questions are still raised, with the same aim of trying to validate the miraculous. However the very essence of God's miraculous work is that it cannot be totally explained. Are we trying to find 'logical' answers instead of accepting that God's work is often beyond our understanding?

Disappearing from the scene

The third question asked by this group of neighbours takes their investigation further. Having heard the healed man's account of the steps he had been told to take, *"He* [Jesus] *told me to go to Siloam and wash,"* they then ask *"Where is this man?"* It is intriguing that Jesus, having directed the man to go and wash, is no longer involved in the verbal exchanges that follow. He re-emerges only at the end when He meets the man again. On a previous occasion Jesus had also left the site of a miracle so that He could not be found: *"Jesus, knowing that they* [the five thousand He had fed with loaves and fishes] *intended to make him king by force, withdrew again to a mountain by himself"* (John 6:15). He recognised the possibility of people's distorted and misguided motives for wanting to encounter Him. Those motives persist today, such as wanting God to prove His existence and power with dramatic interventions. That can be the reason for the question: *"Where is the man?"* But for us it is often the case that God's work takes place in a mundane setting. Are we prioritising a need for dramatic and sensational evidence of God's work, at the expense of being content with His low-key interventions?

Diverging opinion

The theological 'heavyweights' then come into the spotlight. For the Pharisees the day on which the miracle had taken place is a key issue. It did not match up to their doctrinal understanding, as revealed in their statement: *"This man is not from God, for he does not keep the Sabbath"* (verse 16). However this meant that they had a problem which emerges in their follow-up question: *"How can a sinner perform such signs?"* Then, as now, a divergence of opinion was evident: *"So they were divided."*

Needing to clarify the situation the religious leaders carry out an interrogation of the healed man starting with a somewhat leading question: *"What have you to say about him? It was your eyes he opened."* The reply indicates that the man was 'playing it safe.' The Pharisees' agenda, even before it comes out openly, was fairly obvious. Jesus could not be seen as being God. So His miracle had to be discounted. Even so, for the man to say of Jesus, *"He is a prophet,"* is not pointing in the right direction for the religious leaders. This raises an issue that we need to consider. Like those religious leaders are we trying to manage God's ways of working to conform to our own idea of what He should do, and how He should do it?

Final questions

The Pharisees make a further effort to show that no miracle had actually taken place. But when they question the man's parents they make no progress in that respect. His parents simply reply that *"..our son...was born blind..."* They refuse to go down the road of trying to explain how he could now see: *"He is of age; he will speak for himself."* So the final questions are put to the man: *"What did he do to you? How did he open your eyes?"* (verse 26). Having already affirmed: *"One thing I know. I was blind but now I see!"* (verse 25) there is a strong sense of irony in his next reply: *"I have told you already and you did not listen. Why do you want to hear it again? Do you want to become his disciples too?"* The Pharisees cannot handle this response or his final words: *"If this man were not from God, he could do nothing."* They reply angrily before expelling him from the synagogue community. Essentially the religious leaders reject Jesus. But the healed man's response to Him is that of worship and submission (verse 38). Is that yours?

Reflection

1. What steps can you take to be more aware of the work that God is undertaking in your life?
2. How can you develop a greater degree of trust even when you don't understand what God is doing?
3. How can you accept and value the low-key experiences of God, and resist the allure of the 'sensational'?
4. In what ways can you express worship and submission to God in recognition of what He is doing in your life?

Pray: Dear God, please give me a greater sense of trust in You even when I would otherwise ask many questions.

17. Hope

"Jesus called out in a loud voice, 'Lazarus, come out!'" (John 11:43)

Read: John 11:1-44

It presented a powerful image. A daffodil about to break out into flower would not have attracted attention except for one thing. It was located in a patch of earth set amidst the litter, paving stones and busy footfall of a south London street. The caption for this image was bold: 'Hope in unexpected places.'

The leaflet with this message was produced by a group of Christians aiming to help local people get sufficiently numerate, literate and equipped so as to be job-ready and escape the poverty-trap so prevalent in that deprived area.

However that caption is also applicable to each of us, arising from God's ability to miraculously intervene in our lives. Some of the ways in which God-given hope can be experienced is evidenced in the final miracle of Jesus that John records. This is the raising of Lazarus from the dead.

"Hope" is integral to spiritual life, an element of faith: *"Now faith is confidence in what we hope for and assurance about what we do not see"* (Hebrews 11:1). The account in John 11 has only two verses which describe the actual raising of Lazarus (verses 43-44), but there are around 42 verses which express how the hopes and grief of those affected by his death determine their response to this loss.

1. Reaching out

The first aspect of hope is shown in the news that is sent by Lazarus' sisters to Jesus: *"Lord, the one you love is ill"* (verse 3). Martha and Mary are specifically reaching out to Jesus. This is important to note because so often the word ‘hope’ is used in a nebulous or vague way. We ‘hope’ the the weather will improve, that the bus will arrive soon, or that our local football team will win. (The last kind of hope can be a forlorn one if, like me, you follow a club like Leyton Orient.) However the Bible clearly shows that as Christians we can experience hope, not in a hazy and ill-defined way, but as something focused. This was the experience of the Psalmist: *“Why, my soul, are you downcast? Why so disturbed within me? Put your hope in God, for I will yet praise him, my Saviour and my God”* (Psalm 42:5). The Psalmist also explained why he put his hope in God: *“But the eyes of the LORD are on those who fear him, on those whose hope is in* ***his unfailing love****”* (33:18; emphasis added).

2. Refocusing

Jesus, following the sisters’ message, delays His departure and arrives in Bethany four days later, after Lazarus has died. Two conversations then take place. Martha is the first one to talk through what has happened and how she sees that things could have been different: *“Lord, if you had been here my brother would not have died”* (verse 21). She adds her perspective on what now might be hoped for: *“I know he* [Lazarus] *will rise again in the resurrection at the last day.”* But Jesus wants to refocus that perspective and introduce a greater element of hope. He makes a profound statement which constitutes one of the well-known seven *“I am”* declarations: *“I am the resurrection and the life. The one who believes in me will live, even though they die; and whoever lives by believing in me will never die.”* He wants Martha to understand that He has the ultimate say in terms of life and death. He can give hope in the most hopeless of situations, and this entirely refocuses and changes our perspective on what confronts us. The Psalmist again understood this aspect of God’s intervention and how it impacted on him: *"I remain confident of this: I will see the goodness of the LORD in the land of the living. Wait for the LORD; be strong and take heart and wait for the LORD"* (Psalm 27:13-14). We can hope for God's intervention, not only in respect of the life to come, but also in the circumstances of this life.

3. Relating

In Jesus' subsequent conversation with Mary another aspect of hope is revealed. This is a shorter exchange. Mary simply underlines what seemed to be a tragic delay in Jesus' arrival: *"Lord, if you had been here, my brother would not have died"* (verse 32). These words are accompanied by tears, shared by those in the immediate vicinity. Jesus is *"deeply moved"* by this display of grief such that He also weeps. This results in the observation being made by those around, *"See how he loved him."* This reflects the initial contact that had been made with Jesus about Lazarus' condition, the words *"...the one you love.."* showing a close relationship that existed between Jesus and this man and his sisters. It is a reminder that hope is strengthened through a deep relationship with Jesus, and this is integral to His miraculous intervention. The Psalmist describes this link between relationship and hope: *"The LORD delights in those who fear him, who put their hope in his unfailing love"* (Psalm 147:11).

4. Response

A final conversation then takes place. It is not clear whether Jesus overhears the comment that was made by onlookers at this point (or senses it anyway): *"Could not he who opened the eyes of the blind man have kept this man from dying?"* (verse 37). The miraculous giving of sight to the man who had been born blind has clearly made an impact (see John 9). In that atmosphere of despair and hopelessness Jesus steps into the limelight and issues a clear command: *"Take away the stone."* This is said as He faces the cave where Lazarus' body has been laid. Martha's response is to point out that after four days of interment the body would be in a state of decomposition. But Jesus reminds her of His power, *"Did I not tell you that if you believe, you will see the glory of God?"* So the stone is taken away. The experience of hope often requires a response undertaken in faith, listening to what God is saying. Jesus calls out in a loud voice, *"Lazarus, come out!"* The power of those words is evident: *"The dead man came out, his hands and feet wrapped with strips of linen, and a cloth round his face."*

Hope is integral to the miraculous intervention of God. Even when hope is lost God can work to generate it, as the apostle Paul found when he was on a storm-battered ship that was about to break up. Everyone on board had given up hope, but Paul had experienced a divine visitation assuring the miraculous survival of everyone with him. His words reflected the hope that was subsequently realised: *"So keep up your courage, men, for I have faith in God that it will happen just as he told me"* (Acts 27:25). Hope, arising from the miraculous intervention of God, can be experienced in dark places and situations, even where you may be at this moment.

Reflection

1. In what ways can you reach out to Jesus with a sense of hope in a way that is more real and definite?
2. How can you better focus on the way that God sees things and how He wants to intervene in your life?
3. What steps can you take to deepen your relationship with Jesus?
4. What is God saying to you that reassures you that with Him there is always hope in dark places?

Pray: Thank You Lord Jesus that when I face adversity hope can arise in your miraculous intervention.

18. Ticking boxes?

"When she heard about Jesus, she came up behind him in the crowd and touched his cloak." (Mark 5:27)

Read: Mark 5:25-34

She is someone who doesn't tick any boxes. Many of Jesus' miraculous interventions recorded in the Gospels have common features. But the incident of the woman who is healed simply by touching Jesus' cloak has none of these elements. No-one has initiated this healing by bringing, introducing or telling Jesus about the woman. She has no face-to-face encounter with Him preceding the healing. And the woman's healing is not effected by Jesus' word of command, instruction or any other specific action on His part.

A condition

In fact a unique feature of this intervention is that there is no indication of Jesus having any inkling of the healing about to happen. He also does not know the identity of the person to whom His power has been released until after the healing has taken place. There is a significant reason why the woman avoids any face-to-face approach or contact with Jesus. This is because of her condition: *"...subject to bleeding for twelve years."* God had laid down regulations for living and lifestyle through Moses many years previously which included: *"When a woman has a discharge of blood for many days at a time other than her monthly period or has a discharge that continues beyond her period, she will be unclean as long as she has the discharge"* (Leviticus 15:25). It means that the woman would be categorised as *"unclean."*

Spending all her money on doctors to remedy her condition had been unsuccessful - instead her condition had become worse. Also, on account of being *"unclean,"* she was deemed a social outcast and was barred from entering the temple to engage in worshipping God with other people.

A contrast

The contrast of her situation with someone else needing Jesus' intervention at that time is a strong one. When she approaches Jesus He is on His way to the house of Jairus, one of the synagogue leaders. This man's daughter is close to death and so Jairus has pleaded with Jesus to come and put His hands on her so that she will be healed and live. Here is a respected member of the community, upfront and publicly presenting his case, asking for specific intervention.

A conjecture

But the woman cannot tick any of these boxes. There is only one thing that she can do. She had previously conjectured: *"If I just touch his clothes, I will be healed."* This had the vital advantage of her remaining anonymous, helped by the fact that a *"large crowd"* was accompanying Jesus as He walked along. So she deliberately comes behind Jesus and touches His cloak, a touch that's done in faith. The result is instantaneous and total: *"Immediately her bleeding stopped and she felt in her body that she was freed from her suffering"* (Mark 5:29).

A consequence ... something more

But something else happens. This is not what she has anticipated! Realising that *"power had gone out from him"* Jesus promptly turns round and asks *"Who touched my clothes?"* The disciples' response that contact in such a crowded environment is inevitable does not bring closure. Jesus continues to look amongst the crowd until the woman, knowing what has happened to her, comes and falls at His feet. Jairus, the religious leader, had earlier approached Jesus in that same way. But this woman is overwhelmed by the enormity of what she has done and the outcome. So she comes *"trembling with fear."* In addition, for a woman to speak out in public was a non-starter in that culture. So there are no boxes that she can tick to regularise what she has done or is now doing ... but she tells Jesus everything anyway.

The woman's acknowledgement before Jesus of her condition, and her desperate action to receive healing, results in a 'something more' experience. Jesus also brings healing to her battered and broken spirit which had resulted from her physical affliction. He addresses her as *"Daughter."* This is the only time in the Gospels that Jesus speaks to anyone in this way, bringing into focus how God sees her - a beloved, chosen and deeply cared-for child of God. Jesus also speaks words of peace to her, *"Shalom,"* denoting wholeness and well-being. She had approached Jesus simply to touch his clothes, believing that this would be sufficient for her physical healing. But she comes away not only experiencing physical healing, but also having her inner being now touched by Jesus' words of affirmation: *"Go in peace and be freed from your suffering"* (Mark 5:34).

Confined

The late Jenny Rees-Larcombe was a committed Christian who was having to handle life from the confines of a wheelchair. Also afflicted with depression, spiritual darkness and unanswered prayer, she set out to help others grappling with similar issues, and eventually founded an organisation called 'Beauty from ashes.' During this time many mature and experienced Christians prayed with her for healing but no intervention from God resulted. So when, on one occasion following a meeting at which she had been the speaker, she was approached by someone who offered to pray for her, Jenny was not confident that anything would happen. This was especially so because the girl had only recently become a Christian and had no experience of praying in such a situation. No boxes were being ticked. But despite Jenny's hesitation she let the girl pray .... and then immediately experienced God's miraculous healing, being able to discard her wheel chair.

The requirement, conscious or otherwise, of ticking boxes in order to experience God's intervention can be a feature of church life and ministry. There is a tendency to feel that laid-down structures, protocols and practices have to be followed in order to experience God's response to various life issues such as healing, provision, guidance and gifting. But like the woman, we may find that we simply don't tick these boxes. However, like her, we have one thing that we can do. Focus on Jesus. He is the source of all power, and His love has no limit. What boxes can you leave unticked as you focus on God and seek something more?

Reflection

1. In what ways did the woman's untreatable condition act as a driver to her coming to Jesus? How can such a scenario be relevant to you?
2. Why was it important that the woman did not try to copy other people's ways of approaching Jesus? How can other people's experiences of God's intervention prove a distraction to you when you come to Him?
3. Why was it necessary for the woman to consider her course of action before approaching Jesus? How can that apply to you?
4. The woman had not anticipated Jesus' response to her approach. What does that teach you about being ready to listen to what He might say to you?

Pray: Lord Jesus, whatever boxes I may seem unable to tick, help me to focus on You as I bring You my need of Your intervention.

19. Confrontation

"Then he told her, 'For such a reply, you may go; the demon has left your daughter.'" (Mark 7:29)

Read: Mark 7:24-30

Whilst working in the civil service my line manager on one occasion announced that he was signing me up for 'assertiveness' training. I refused to attend the course. It was therefore evident that it was not actually needed!

Some situations can bring out unanticipated assertiveness. This was shown by a woman who approached Jesus because of her daughter's condition. At this point in Jesus' travels He had withdrawn from the public eye and had gone about 30 miles north of Galilee to the region of Tyre and Sidon. This was the only recorded occasion when he went into territory that was completely outside Jewish influence. This was clearly no coincidental or unintentional move as He then *"entered a house and did not want anyone to know it..."* However His 'time out' did not materialise *"...yet he could not keep His presence secret"* (Mark 7:24). This is the setting for the account of a woman whose desperate situation brought out an unanticipated response. The way she confronted Jesus, in an assertive way, resulted in a miracle. The details about her situation and actions are relevant to us.

1. Plight

The woman's first words to Jesus reveal her plight: *"My daughter is demon-possessed and suffering terribly"* (Matthew 15:22). Mark's account records the girl as being a *"little daughter...possessed by an impure spirit"* (Mark 7:25). The indication that the daughter was not an adult adds to the sense of vulnerability and helplessness overwhelming the mother who cared deeply for her child but was powerless to do anything.

The nature of the affliction is clearly described - *"demon possession"* - a diagnosis that may sit uncomfortably with a modern day audience including Bible-believers. The Gospel writers had no difficulty in identifying physical conditions such as blindness, deafness, paralysis and leprosy which afflicted people and to whom Jesus brought specific healing. But this girl's condition was markedly not in that category. The mother specifically requested Jesus to *"**drive** the demon out of her daughter"* (Mark 7:26; emphasis added). The word *"drive"* in its original form denoted a forceful casting out or ejection, and would not be applicable to healing a physical ailment. Jesus had previously engaged in a heated discussion with religious leaders about demon possession and how it was to be handled, and He had used the same word (*"drive;"* Matthew 12:22-29). Neither the existence nor intrusion of demonic beings was questioned on that occasion. Although contemporary science may influence the church to discard this concept, Jesus' ministry showed that He regarded demonic activity as real and something that needed to be confronted.

2. Perception

The mother's response to her daughter's dire condition is also stated: *"A Canaanite woman from that vicinity came to him, crying out, 'Lord, Son of David, have mercy on me!'" "...came and fell at his feet...She begged Jesus ..."* (Matthew 15:22; Mark 7:25, 26). Even though she was not a Jew or recorded as being a follower of the Jewish faith (Mark states that she was a Greek, born in Syria Phoenicia) by using the term 'Son of David' she perceives Jesus to be the Jewish promised Messiah. But this perception is evident not only in her words (*"crying out...begged"*) but also in her actions. She *"fell at his feet"* showing her reverence and dependence on Him. It also shows her belief in Him having power to intervene.

3. Persistence

However Jesus' disciples were not impressed by this woman's persistence: *"So his disciples ... urged him, 'Send her away, for she keeps crying out after us'"* (Matthew 15:23). In any case at this stage Jesus' response to her is presented as non-committal: *"Jesus did not answer a word"* (verse 23). But then He makes an unambiguous statement: *"I was sent only to the lost sheep of Israel"* (verse 24). The woman, although not a Jew or a *"lost sheep,"* is still not put off. She kneels before Jesus and asks: *"Lord, help me!"* (Matthew 15:25).

In response to her words Jesus adds to what He's just said about His work being only among the Jews: *"It is not right to take the children's bread and toss it to the dogs"* (Mark 7:27). Mark's account also emphasises the priority of God's people over others in Jesus' work: *"First let the children eat all they want ... for it is not right to take the children's bread and toss it to the dogs"* (Mark 7:27). This rebuttal would seem to bring the matter to an end.

However it's at this point that her persistence moves into unanticipated action. She confronts Jesus with an argument to back up her case! She initially admits that Jesus is correct about the Jews being His priority: *"Yes it is Lord"* (Matthew 15:27), but then she homes-in on the word *"dogs"* which Jesus had just used. The kind of dog to which Jesus referred was not the scavenging, running-loose variety, seen in the streets, but the domesticated pet found in people's homes. The woman argues that this pet dog is actually allowed to devour crumbs that might fall from the family meal table. Her belief that she qualified for Jesus' intervention if only on the basis of those *"crumbs"* brought the response she desperately needed. Jesus agreed with her point: *"Woman, you have great faith! Your request is granted"* (Matthew 15:28). He did not even have to go to her daughter. His power was such that: *"She went home and found her child on the bed, and the demon gone"* (Mark 7:30).

Pattern

The woman's action in pressing an argument for her case forms part of a pattern. King Jehoshaphat, receiving news of an enemy attack, pointed out to God that He had not allowed the Israelites to occupy the territory of those now invading them (2 Chronicles 20). Similarly King Hezekiah, told of his imminent death, reminded God that he had been faithful to Him (Isaiah 38). Both kings experienced God's intervention - military success and extension of life-span respectively. Abraham also confronted God when informed of Sodom's pending destruction. He pointed out that God's justice would not allow this action if there were even just a few righteous people in the city. Although the destruction took place God first rescued Lot, Abraham's nephew, and his family, from the city (Genesis 18). In pressing God for His miraculous intervention, what would you present as an argument to Him?

Reflection

1. What is the significance of the woman's initial approach to Jesus in begging and falling at His feet? How does that apply to you?
2. The woman evidently disregards the words of Jesus' disciples. Why is it important not to pay attention to the comments of other people when you come to Jesus?
3. How can other peoples' comments be pushed aside?
4. How can you overcome feelings that you may not 'qualify' when asking for God's intervention?

Pray: Jesus, help me to know that you always hear me and that I can argue my case in my prayers to You.

20. Reality check

"When he had spat on the man's eyes and put his hands on him, Jesus asked, 'Do you see anything?'" (Mark 8:23)

Read: Mark 8:22-26

Researchers at the Maryland University in the USA undertook a study in 2013 to determine the number of words normally spoken by a person in a routine day. They established that we speak around twenty thousand words in a 24 hour period. Although this seems a high figure we need to take into account that in a busy social or work environment there are likely to be lots of words flying around!

There is a further aspect of that study. Many of the conversations that generate these words include questions being asked and answered. We probably don't realise the number of these since most of them are insignificant. We even ask ourselves some of them...out loud! 'Where's my phone?' 'What's my PIN?' 'Shall I wear a coat?'

Inconsequential...or important

Most of our questions are directed to those around us and are raised without much thought: 'Will it rain today?' 'What time's the bus?' 'Tea or coffee?' However there are other questions that operate at a deeper level, which are concerned with well-being and are of a more personal nature. 'How are you feeling?' 'Why are you stressed-out? 'What's going on?' Brief questions can open up significant inner concerns.

Another aspect of questions to be taken into account is when they are asked as a means of probing someone for their benefit. 'Why haven't you done your homework?' is a question likely to have been heard when we were at school.

However 'Why didn't you phone me?' 'Where's the money?' 'How could you do this?' are likely to constitute more recent probing words.

Questions from God

What may be surprising is that God is described in the Bible as asking questions. The opening recorded conversation between God and Adam, the first man, comes in the form of His question: *"Where are you?"* (Genesis 3:9). In essence God is asking, 'Why are you hiding from me?'

These words from God formed a pattern but were not designed to fill a gap in His knowledge. He already knew the answers on account of being all-powerful, ever-present and all-knowing. It's like a school teacher asking a student: 'What is the capital city of France?' Clearly the teacher knows the answer but asks the question to challenge the student's knowledge. Is there something further the student needs to address? Almost inevitably this is the reason behind God's questions. People (individuals or groups) need to be made aware of something that they have not previously realised...or have tried to push away. God will not put up with such ignorance or negativity! His questions can have significant implications!

Spitting .... and asking!

The miracle of Jesus bringing sight to a blind man (Mark 8) includes a key question. The man has been brought to Jesus by others who specifically "*begged Jesus to touch him.*" The account, unique to Mark's Gospel, features a means of healing not recorded by any other Gospel writer. Jesus "*spat*" directly onto the the man's eyes. The previous chapter described Him using saliva which He seemingly spat onto His hand and then placed on the tongue of a deaf man who could hardly speak (Mark 7:33). But it is the question to this blind man whom Jesus has led out of the village that is noticeable: "*Do you see anything?*"

Seeing ... but not perfectly

What was the reason for asking it? The man's response is "*I see people; they look like trees walking around.*" This indicates two things. Firstly it suggests that the man had previously been able to see, since he knew what trees looked like and he knew that they were not usually mobile! But secondly, and more importantly, it reveals that his vision was now restored but was not perfect. This is confirmed by the subsequent statement: "*Once more Jesus put his hands on the man's eyes.*" The result is that his sight is totally recovered and he sees everything "*clearly*".

So, unlike other miracles, this healing was not completely effective immediately. Although the time lapse between the first and second touching of the man's eyes by Jesus is probably measured by just a few moments, the initial contact was insufficient. So the question Jesus asked was apparently necessary in order to determine the progress of restoration that the man was experiencing.

A challenge ... and a crisis!

Rather than see this question as a reflection on the degree of divine power that was at work it should also be understood as a challenge to the man. A 'reality check' was required. Was he going to be satisfied with experiencing some degree of sight (rather than nothing at all) however defective it was? The man, perhaps in typical 'British' fashion, could have responded by saying that his sight was now 'fine'! But it certainly was not 'fine'! Perhaps the man could have accepted that things were now 'as good as they could get' and moved on as best he could. He might have anticipated some improvement as time progressed, though Jesus had not presented this possibility.

So the question from Jesus highlighted a critical issue. Was the man prepared to openly acknowledge his present situation and, in so doing, show that he was not satisfied with it? This might have been a step that the man was reticent to take. It could have resulted in him being told to 'be grateful for what you have, so put up with it.' It was only because the man responded honestly that he then received complete healing.

The reason behind Jesus' question is also relevant to us as we face unanswered prayer, or where a miraculous intervention has not fully addressed our need. Is Jesus using such a scenario to bring us to a crisis point? Are we satisfied with where we are, if it is not where we want to be? So we may be challenged to undertake a personal 'reality check'. It is only as we face up to situations that we may experience a further touch from Jesus. Are you ready to be 'real' with Him and experience 'something more'?

Reflection

1. What reasons do you use to try and 'shrug off' incomplete miraculous intervention?
2. What form can a personal 'reality check' actually take?
3. What did the writer of Lamentations 3 find when he faced up to adversity (see verses 13-24)?
4. Why does God not want you to be satisfied with where you are 'at' but encourages you to seek more from Him (see Ephesians 3:26; Jeremiah 33:3; Psalm 103:5)?

Pray: Dear God please help me to be honest with myself, and be ready to bring you all my concerns regarding Your intervention in my life.

One more miracle?

'Miracle on the Hudson.' Actor Tom Hanks starred as Captain 'Sully' Sullenberger in the film depicting an incident in 2009 involving a US Airlines Airbus 320. 'Sully' had just taken off from LaGuardia Airport, New York, when he flew into a flock of Canada geese. Several of these large birds were sucked into the aircraft's two engines, immediately wrecking them, and resulting in loss of all power. The pilot and his first officer realised that they had very few options available to them - they had to land immediately. Flying over the built-up area of New York, 'Sully' prepared to land on the only available space below, the Hudson River!

YouTube presenter, 'Mentour Pilot,' specialising in documentaries for professionals in aeronautics, had no hesitation in describing 'Sully's' subsequent and successful ditching of his aircraft onto the river as a "miracle." He highlighted the combination of particular variable factors - weather conditions, the configuration of the Airbus, the captain's immediate response, the stretch of river where they ditched - along with other technical aspects, that qualified this event as being a "miracle." The 155 passengers and crew who all survived the emergency landing would not have argued with that description!

Rebuke

So it's a challenge to our faith as Christians that we doubt or are reticent to accept that God can and will work in our lives in miraculous ways. If Godless cynics and sceptics, including hardened professionals in the world of aviation, have no reticence - without acknowledging God - in applying the word "miracle" to an outcome which would not have seemed possible, we should be even more prepared to expect such intervention. Other notable events have seen secular historians also apply this term: the 'Miracle of Dunkirk' (1940) and the 'Miracle of the Marne' (the 1914 First World War battle preventing the capture of Paris by armies of the Central Powers) are two examples.

Realisation

However, accepting that God is the One *"who performs miracles"* is not only recognising that He intervenes in the circumstances that challenge and confuse us. It is to realise that there is 'something more' that we need to understand. God works miracles not only to reveal His total power and authority, but also as a means of deepening our relationship with Him. The Apostle Paul indicated this in his passage on the subject of love. *"If I have a faith that can move mountains, but do not have love, I am nothing"* (1 Corinthians 13:2). The miraculous intervention of God in people's lives described in the Bible, many of whom were ordinary men and women getting on with life as best they could, showed more than His life-changing ability. Behind each of these incidents was a revelation of His care and compassion to those in a sin-darkened and tormented world.

God's intervention, however undemonstrative or low-key, is a means by which His love can be revealed to each of us. His love is unending and unfathomable. It is *"new every morning"* and *"unfailing."* So be alert, expectant and grateful for God to work miraculously. But also be open to experience a greater awareness of His love for you. Because there is always something more!

Further Reading other Bible-Bish-Books by this author

'Are you asking me, God?' (ISBN 9781916405400)
This explores 31 of over 300 questions asked by Jesus recorded in the Gospels, showing how they also relate to us.

'Gathering up ducklings?' (ISBN 9781916405417)
God's encouragement is vital - looking at some Bible passages in which this is brought, prefaced by a 'parable' about ducklings!

'Approaching an open gate' (ISBN 9781916405424)
Exploring the invitations, opportunities and new phases God gives us, presented in the Bible through the images of 'gates.'

'End of the Road?' (ISBN 9781916405448)
Looking at God's intervention through Nehemiah to bring restoration to people's lives, and applying this to us.

'The hollow of His Hand' (ISBN 9781916405462)
The term God's 'hand' is often used in the Bible, and this book looks at some examples and how they connect with ourselves.

'Finding your feet?' (ISBN 9781916405486)
Our journey through life is often pictured in the Bible by reference to our feet - walking, standing, running, slipping. This book describes God's intervention in helping us to 'find our feet.'